Seeing Jesus with New Eyes

Gospel Reflections for the Journey

*Happy Birthday
Sandra*

*From Cynthia
2019*

Larry Warner

barefooted publishing
Oceanside, CA 92054

Scripture quotations marked MSG are taken from THE MESSAGE, copyright © 1993, 2002, 2018 by Eugene H. Peterson. Used by permission of NavPress. All rights reserved. Represented by Tyndale House Publishers, Inc.

Cover Design: Christine Smith
Image: Upsplash
Interior Design: Debbi Stocco

Library of Congress Cataloging-in-Publication Data
Author Name: Warner, Larry, 1955-
Title: Seeing Jesus with New Eyes: Gospel Reflections for the Journey
Description: Oceanside: barefooted publishing, 2019
Identifiers: LCCN 2019911035 (print) ISBN 9780998218670 (paper) ISBN 9780998218632 (ebook)
LC records available at http//lccn.lov.gov/2018907384

ISBN 978-0-9982186-7-0 (paper)
ISBN 978-0-9982186-3-2 (ebook)

Acknowledgment
"Priestly Sprinkler" was previously published in *San Diego Poetry Annual*, Garden Oak Press, Rainbow CA: 2019 (p. 75)

DEDICATION

This book is dedicated to Celia Bradley and Carol Kierulff. These two wonderfully gracious, wise, talented and generous sisters in Christ were instrumental in the starting of b.

Celia worked tirelessly to establish b as an official legal entity, as well as providing ongoing encouragement and practical, detail-oriented work behind the scenes. She gave spiritual direction to many as b grew. She was extremely helpful in getting *Journey with Jesus* written and was someone whose wisdom and insight I was able to count and depend on.

Carol was a prayer warrior, supporting b as God led her to do so and sharing with me the things God shared with her as she prayed for b and for me. Early on in the ministry of b, she shared a vision God had given her about b. She saw arrows originating in San Diego and going out from there in all directions, spreading throughout the United States and around the world. This was something I did not even think possible, but through books, videos and spiritual direction, it has happened and is continuing to happen. In everything I did, I knew Carol was praying for b and for me, and this provided great solace and deepened my ability to trust in and depend on God.

I'm so grateful that God choose to put each of these wise and godly people in my life.

TABLE OF CONTENTS

Section Three: Jesus' Death and Resurrection

Preface

This book is an outgrowth of my love for Jesus and the scriptures. For over forty-five years, God has used this love to mold me into the person I have become, the person God created and called me to be.

The Gospels are my favorite. I love entering into the stories alongside Jesus and the disciples, much like a child would imaginatively enter a story, and I have long desired to write a book that facilitates that same entry for the reader—an engagement of heart as well as head. Hence this book.

The poetic form of this book grew out of a comment I heard a number of years ago, a throwaway line by a speaker that landed on me like a grand piano plummeting from the window of a high rise to the street below. The impact of this sentence created countless previously unimagined possibilities for creative interpretation: "I believe that all theology should be expressed via poetry." I had journaled poetry as therapy after the death of my son, Nathan (see my book *Journey with Grief*), but these words opened to me a brand-new kind of poetic engagement. Poetry presented the possibility of joining together heart and head when interacting with scripture and biblical truth, and so I began to practice hearing and telling the stories and teachings of Jesus through a poetic lens.

Now if even the mention of poetry makes you uncomfortable, I need to set the record straight. I am not a lover of all poetry, nor am I a fan of overtly rhyming poems. My head is not turned by a sonnet, and I am admittedly lost in the imagery of many of the great poetic works. I am an everyday, ordinary person who writes poetry in a style called free verse. It lets me write as I wish in terms of length of lines, punctuation, mixed metaphors—I like no-holds-barred poetry, a person-on-the-street style of poetry, poems for non-poets. The poetry in this book is not astounding, clever or enigmatic. It flows from understanding Jesus and the scriptures as alive and dynamic and offers the invitation to engage both with a childlike playfulness.

What follows is my theology of poetry and my hope for all who choose to interact with scripture anew.

THE POET

I long to write
of longings, desires, musings
which shred souls
    captivate minds
        send hearts soaring
            foster greater awareness.

I long to hear
reflections of poets and mystics
critics and teachers
journalists and philosophers
for in hearing their voices,
I discover my own.

I long to hear the heartbeat of God.

The craft, the gift, the burden of poetry
is found when one is not looking;
it seeps to the surface
like an artesian spring
or gushes forth like a Yellowstone geyser.

The poet a midwife
birthing new awareness,
new life.

I long to be lost crafting poetry,
mountains of time given to it,
entering its deserts and oases,
harnessing the fluid power of creativity,
hunting the word, phrase, image,
that will unlock a heart,
free a soul.

I long to be in an ocean of silence,
in an unhurried and spacious universe,
present with and to the crowd of witnesses
who choose to be naked—
open, waiting, listening,
pen in hand.

INTRODUCTION

This collection of meditations was written for those hungering for a deeper encounter with the gospel narratives and teachings of Jesus. Familiar passages have been reworked in poetic style in order to help the reader engage both heart and head, and each is followed by a short reflective prompt for pondering. My hope is that you will see the person of Jesus through new eyes and be able to enter into these marvelous stories from scripture in a lively, playful and dynamic way. I pray the Holy Spirit will provide tiny fissures of insight opening into chasms of creativity and canyons of change that will awaken your heart and mind anew to the adventure that is living Jesus.

The book is divided into three sections: *Jesus' Birth to Baptism, Jesus' Teachings and Ministry* and *Jesus' Death and Resurrection*. You can choose to read the 117 meditations in any order that seems natural: journeying straight through, randomly choosing or taking a section at a time. You may want to explore the birth to baptism section during Advent season, the cross and resurrection passages during the Lenten season. There are also two indexes that link poems to major themes and to the scriptures from which they are taken; an appendix provides a list of reflections for Palm Sunday through Easter Sunday.

As you enter into this book, I hope it will be meaningful to you in the following ways:

1. Your heart and mind will be expanded as to the person and teaching of Jesus.

2. You will know and love Jesus more deeply by walking with Jesus.

3. The flames of your own God-given creativity will be freed to engage and enjoy.

4. As your knowledge and love of Jesus deepens, you will be inspired to be the person God has created and called you to be.

5. Hearing the words and teachings of Jesus differently, playfully and passionately will enrich your life and cause you to embrace the freedom and adventure that is walking with Jesus.

MINING THE MEDITATIONS

This brief chapter is meant to help you open to and partner with God as you spend time in the meditations that follow. Don't feel you need to read one daily, as no structure is intended. The goal is not to complete a poem daily, nor even to get through the entire book. My prayer is that these poetic expressions will connect you with God in new and deeper ways, and that your faith and life will be enriched because of them.

Some first steps:

1. Begin by getting into a comfortable position. Take a couple of deep breaths and confidently remember that God is with you and within you; then offer yourself and this time to God.

2. Interact with the material slowly and thoughtfully, paying attention to the words and/or phrases to which you are drawn or that incite resistance; be aware of the emotions stirring within you.

3. Take time to linger over and savor the words and/or phrases that caught your attention (drawn to, resistant toward) and the associated feelings, pondering the reminder, invitation, challenge or encouragement God is revealing to you (use the acronym RICE as a prompt, if it's helpful).

Resistance

Whenever you become aware of resistance, take time to pause and ponder. Resistance is a gift from God that invites you into deeper discoveries concerning God and/or yourself. Ask God to help you discern the source of this resistance. What does it reveal about your image, level of belief, love and trust of God? What does it tell you about your sense of self, your identity? Pause, ponder and unpack your resistance, as over time the results can be life-changing.

4. Take time to journal about your discoveries, insights and feelings. Feel free to journal in your own way—electronically, pen and paper, writing a single word or filling an entire page. Journal as you can, not as you cannot, while being open to the invitation to be creative, to bring a playfulness to your journaling (colors, drawings, pictures, crayons, paint).

Perfectionism

If you are a perfectionist or a recovering perfectionist, please be on guard. If you begin to feel stress about "doing it right" or you begin to hear an internal voice of shame or condemnation, stop and ask God to help you be gracious and patient with yourself. These voices are not coming from God but are lies that distract you, taking your attention away from God rather than toward God. Remember there is no condemnation in Christ.

5. Each meditation includes reflection questions, prompts, and sometimes practices, which are designed to help you continue to explore. These prompts are for you to use or not as you choose. If you sense a deep engagement with God through a particular meditation, you can also use the questions separately. The

prompts and practices are there for you only if you find them helpful, but don't feel the need to include them.

6. Take something with you from your time with God. As your meditation comes to an end, choose to carry with you throughout your day a thought or new insight that surfaced during your time, and consider it a gift from God for the day. This is a form of meditation developed in the Middle Ages called *nosegay*, which refers to a small bunch of flowers. It's also reminiscent of the practice of putting petals in one's pocket during the black plague, as in the child's poem, "pocket full of posies." As the stench of sickness and dying grew stronger, the survivors would remove the flowers from their pockets and hold them to their noses to disguise the overpowering smell of death. So this God-originated nosegay reminds you of God's presence, involvement, caring concern and resources; carry the freshness of the Spirit of God with you into your day.

7. Finally, every so often, take a few moments to review the truths and insights you and God discovered together. Reflecting on your past provides an opportunity to consider themes, recurring words and insights that emerged, exploring how they may be invitations from God.

Use of Scripture

There is a passage or passages connected to almost every meditation. The listed passage(s) provided the inspiration for that day's reflection. As part of your time you may want to look at the passage(s) before or after—even the day before or the day after—you read the meditation. This practice can help cultivate your own creativity and well as provide an additional opportunity for you to receive from God through the passage(s).

SECTION ONE

JESUS' BIRTH TO BAPTISM

GOD HAS SPOKEN

Since the beginning
God has spoken.
God the articulate artisan
creative communicator
wordless whisperer
thundering proclaimer
eloquent orator
powerful pontificator
masterful storyteller
clever poet.
Employing a myriad of methods
to communicate truth—
burning bushes
braying donkeys
menacing messengers
a gentle breeze
trees, sunsets
crashing waves
a star in the sky
a babe in a manger
Jesus
overturned tables
water turned to wine
thousands fed
raising the dead
calming storms
blind healed
feet washed
an image on a coin
lines in the sand
dreams
parables, pounding nails

a cross
an empty tomb
a piece of bread
a cup of wine
letters penned
the Bible
the Spirit—

God is speaking.

What might you add to the list above? What does this list communicate about God? How do you typically hear God?

Today as you read and reflect, what, if anything, might God be communicating to you? How do you know it is God? As you continue through your day, seek to listen for the communications of God in expected and unexpected places.

LIGHT AND LIFE

(JOHN 1:3-14)

The Light shone brightly,
that Light that brought Life
Life giving Life
adventure, mystery, power
power to reconcile, renew,
offer others Life
not ordinary life but
Life flowing from God
Life transforming people, nations, the world.

This Light that was Life
Creator of all seen and unseen
moving into our neighborhood
walking among us
full of grace and truth
God fleshed out for all to see
yet unrecognized, ignored—
betrayed, mocked, killed.

The darkness seeking to eliminate the Light,
but the Light still brings Life—
not ordinary life but
adventure, mystery,
power to reconcile, renew,
offer Life,
life flowing from God to others
life of faith that moves mountains, walks on water
life of love that speaks in deeds
life of hope, perspective, endurance,
in times of struggle, pain, sorrow,
during the agony of dying dreams.
The Life-Light continues to shine,
the darkness unable to extinguish it.

Which words used above would you say describe your God-given life? Which do you desire to embrace and experience more fully? When are the times in your life you're most aware of the light of God within you? Ask God to show you the elements of your life that may be diminishing your light. Please remember, this is about awareness, not condemnation, and awareness is the beginning of transformation. Now take a moment to thank God for the life God has given you, is fostering in you.

A New Leaf

(Luke 1:26-38)

"May it be so"
and Mary's previous
hopes, dreams, imagined life,
drop like autumn leaves,
still beautiful
but no longer living.

One by one they drop
even as new life grows within,
the old making room
to embrace the new,
but not yet spring,
a cold winter ahead.

She must tell Joseph,
family, friends,

Still she lets them drop,
believing, trusting God.
May it be so!

Reflect on your level of willingness to say yes to God—"may it be so." Where in your life do you struggle to say yes? What dreams, desires, current realities would be most difficult for you to let go of, step away from? What new life may God be seeking to birth within you? What would it look like, feel like, for you to pray "may it be so"?

THE INVITED ONES

(LUKE 1:26-45, 2:8-20)

A celebratory occasion
by personal invitation,
to a select few—probably

not the ones you would think.

The first was a personal invite
to a young female teen, Mary,
delivered by an angel—
not some chubby cherub
but God's chosen messenger
assuring the invited one,
"Do not be afraid."

The next recipient
an older women,
her unborn baby and the Holy Spirit
sharing the news.

The invitations continued—
herald angels invite unheralded shepherds,
a heavenly star summons three Gentiles.
Yet, the religious establishment received no
save-the-date postcard, no invitation—
the powers that be were left guessing
the details of this earthshaking,
history-shaping, life-altering event—
the baby shower for Mary.

The guest list—
women, herders, Gentiles,
the marginalized, minimized, less-than,
those deemed unimportant.

God choosing these humble outsiders
to attend to the birth of God's only son.

Jesus continues this tradition—
calling the outcast, seeking the oppressed,
blind, prisoners, marginalized,
the lame, deaf, lepers,
tax collectors, Samaritans,
Gentiles and women,
the poor in spirit, those who mourn
to gather at his table,
to attend his marriage supper.

What do these lines reveal about the heart of God toward the religious, powerful, disenfranchised? How does God's hospitality compare to yours? Be open to God's prompting and look for an opportunity to invite someone into the events (big and small) of your life.

LIGHT WAS LIFE

(JOHN 1:3-5, 1:9-13, 3:19, 8:12)

The light shines out
    a tiny flicker
    newborn yet eternal
    the Light of Life
The darkness not comprehending
    this Life-Light
The darkness not overcoming
    this Life-Light
People choosing darkness
    over Life-Light
Giving themselves to the deeds of darkness
Turning themselves away from enlightenment
Crucifying the Light

BUT not all

Some recognized the Light
Some received Life
Transformed and free
    to be and become
    the persons God created them to be
Reborn, not blood-begotten
    not flesh, not sex-conceived
begotten by God in love, free
    to serve, to become, to be
    to live as light in a darkened world
Light penetrating their darkness
    bringing fullness of life.

As you reflect on the world around you, where do you see 1) light penetrating the darkness—pause and give thanks, 2) people bringing light into the darkness—pause and pray for those individuals, 3) the darkness seeking to extinguish the light—pause and bring those things, institutions and people before God.

Explore your own life, asking where you see your God-light shining most brightly. Reflect on and celebrate the ways you have been or are being transformed, freed, by Life with Jesus.

ANNA AND SIMEON

(Luke 2:25-38)

Faithful followers
wanting, waiting,
trusting,
believing

Fervent followers
steadfast, day after day
knowing, not knowing
when faith would become sight

Fortified followers
love fueling their resolve
belief belying contrary voices
within and without

Fluid followers
in tune with the Spirit
two feathers
floating on the breath of God

Favored followers
holding, blessing baby God
cooing, caressing, cuddling

Faithfulness fulfilled.

Anna and Simeon demonstrated an extraordinary faith in God. Which stanza best describes your walk with God? Ask God to strengthen your faith where needed and celebrate the areas in your life where you are being faithful to God. How might the Spirit be moving in you to become a feather in your own life? When have there been moments you experienced this lighthearted peace, confidence or cooperation with God?

WOMB, WOUNDS AND TOMB

(LUKE 2:6-7, JOHN 19:34, MATTHEW 28:1-7)

Jesus' entry into the world
gushing water,
flow of blood—
God Incarnate, baby
bringing Light, Life, Love.

Jesus' birth announcing
proclaiming, declaring
God's all-in love,
immersed in the messiness of life.

Jesus' departure from the world
gushing water,
flow of blood—
making Light, Life and Love
available to the world.

Jesus' death announcing
proclaiming, declaring
God loves—an active love
steeped in the messiness of life.

Mary's womb
our pathway for Life and Love
Jesus, our Lover
willing to lay down his life for Love.

Jesus' wounds —
womb and pathway
to God's everlasting love
available to all.

The womb, the wounds, the empty tomb,
announcement, proclamation, declaration,

God is love, God loves you,
Love wins.

What is birthed from the womb of Jesus' wounds? Reflect on your wounds; what has been birthed within you and through you because of what you have suffered? What does this communicate to you about God's use of suffering?

Jesus in the Temple

(John 2:12-17)

Jesus stays behind
mother, father, family
depart Jerusalem
heading home

Jesus, about twelve, remains
entering the synagogue
(His Father's House)
the learned men amused
by the presence of one so young

The scholars and scribes
ask him questions
and marvel at the replies, insights
of one so young

One day they will
again pepper him with
questions—no longer amused
by his answers but cut to the quick

One day they will plot to kill him
they will have him arrested
demand he be crucified

One day they will stand near
as nails are driven through his flesh
as he hangs upon a cross
jeering him, mocking him

Today they pat him on the
head—celebrate the great
knowing in one so young

But this boy will become a man
the Messiah, the Son of God
and these men will be threatened

their knowledge, standing challenged
on that day will any remember this day
the day his answers thrilled them
the day their hearts burned within

─────────────────────────────

The Pharisees easily engaged with twelve-year-old Jesus, but later found Him threatening. In what areas in your life may you be too comfortable with Jesus? In what areas in your life may Jesus be wanting to challenge/expand your thinking, your beliefs about Jesus?

JOHN THE BAPTIZER

(MATTHEW 3:1-12, JOHN 3:30)

I was a desert dweller,
camel-hair-wearing, locust-eating,
road-paving prophet.

I fasted from food and drink,
my voice in the wilderness
proclaiming another's coming.

I baptized Him, as He insisted,
witnessed the heavens open
heard the Voice and knew—my purpose fulfilled.

The Promised One had arrived,
God's kingdom come,
God among us clothed in flesh.

My role diminished as His intensified.
(I knew my purpose, and I knew His!)

Still challenging authority,
imprisoned, beheaded,
I died as I lived.

Proclaiming God,
preaching repentance,
preparing the way.

(owning who I was and who I was not)

John knew who he was and who he was not, and he chose to own who he was. Consider John stepping aside to "make way for Jesus." Have you ever had to set yourself aside/sacrifice your own glory or recognition to prepare the way for another? What's that been like? Who are you—what are your God-given gifts? What are the good works God has uniquely prepared for you to do (Ephesians 2:10)?

This Is My Beloved Son

(Matthew 3:17; 4:3, 4:6; 17:5)

Born a bastard
son of an unwed mother
object of ridicule and shame

"This is My Son, whom I love,
with Him I am well pleased."

Strengthening words
sustaining words
a needed knowing
as his ministry begins

Jesus has done nothing yet—
No water turned to wine
No calming of storms
No healings, no miracles

Yet the heavens opened
a dove descended and God spoke
ontological truth
a declaration of identity, of being, of actuality

A truth soon challenged
by Satan, by the Pharisees,
by others time and again.

"This is My Son, whom I love,
with Him I am well pleased."

These words repeated again
before the cross—words that
empower and fortify Jesus' resolve—
through the abuse, persecutions, attacks,
false accusations, all the way to the Garden

"not my will but your will be done"
to the Cross
"Father, into your hands I commit my Spirit."

"This is My Son, whom I love,
with Him I am well pleased."

Jesus sought to live a God-honoring life. Given the realities of His mission and ministry, what impact do you think God's declaration, "You are My beloved Son," had on Him? What affirmations have you heard in your life from God? How do these shape and inform how you live? Invite God to speak God's love over you and into you; what do you hear, feel and notice?

THUNDER AND LIGHTNING

(MARK 1:4-8, LUKE 4:18-19)

Thunder in the desert,
making known the rumblings of God,
rattling the religious,
calling all to repentance,
making way for the One to come.

Lightning from heaven,
the power/presence of God—
striking the earth,
setting hearts ablaze,
splitting open souls,
setting captives free.

An illuminating life offering,
sight giving light—
revealing, releasing, restoring,
new relational possibilities
with God, self, and others.

What feels exciting, fulfilling and engaging about a life lived with God? In which areas of your life is God inviting you to experience greater freedom? What might God be seeking to reveal and/or restore in your life? Spend some time sharing your thoughts with God.

JESUS

(MATTHEW 4:1; JOHN 4:34, 5:19, 5:30, 8:28, 12:49, 14:10)

Jesus—fully God, fully man
yielded, dependent
working in concert with God
reliant on God
led by the Spirit—
submissive, subservient, obedient
trusting, believing, humble.
His will—subdued, restrained, controlled,
surrendered, relinquished (denial of self)
nothing of his own initiative
joining in the work of God
speaking what he hears from God
sustained and fortified by God's love.

yet not
resigned, stoic, fatalistic, apathetic—

but engaged with, relationally connected
to God—looking, listening, waiting
responding to God's initiatives
implementing God's plans
fleshing out the life we are invited to live—
yielded, dependent
working in concert with God
reliant on God
connected to God
led by the Spirit
submissive, subservient, obedient
trusting, believing
your will not my will
life sustained and fortified by God's love.

What does it look like to live a life sustained and fortified by God's love? Do those words describe your life? Which of these words, "yielded, dependent, submissive, subservient, obedient, trusting, believing," do you feel the most resistance toward? What may God be inviting you to join God in doing, saying? How does God's love for you sustain and fortify your life, inform and shape your choices? What might God be asking you to add/subtract from your life that would help you to engage with God and connect to God more consistently?

Stop, Look and Listen

Having reached the end of this section, take some time to go back and review your journal using one or more of the prompts below. You may want to do this over a few days.

Word/Phrase

Write the words/phrases/questions that stood out to you in the previous reflections, thoughts that drew you in or caused resistance, affected you positively or negatively, moved you in some way. Try using different colored pens to represent different emotions. Pay attention to and make note of your feelings, listening for the invitations or challenges from God.

Exploring Themes

Attempt to discover what message(s) God has for you. What might God be inviting or challenging you to embrace, live into? If a particular theme surfaces, consider the nature of it. Is it more of an invitation (something you long for and welcome) or a challenge (something to overcome)?

What do you notice about Jesus through these poems and questions? Does anything surprise you? How might your feelings toward or your experience of Jesus be shifting, expanding, deepening?

SECTION TWO

JESUS' TEACHINGS AND MINISTRY

JESUS 2.0: UPGRADE MY JESUS?

(COLOSSIANS 1:15-20, ROMANS 11:33-36)

Is it time for a system upgrade?
Updates are available:
new capacities, capabilities
waiting, beckoning, calling.

I hesitate;
horror stories of current programs unsupported,
favorite applications incompatible,
regular procedures rearranged.

I like my tried and true
operating system, interface,
existing configurations.
No need to change!

Seeking refuge in the status quo,
comfort in God's word, my theology,
Jesus the same,
yesterday, today and forever!

I click *not now.*

Ignore the infinite reality,
God's incomprehensible character,
the unexplored depths,
riches, wisdom and knowledge of God.
Unable to fathom the more.

I like my current Jesus,
comfortable and knowable,
working just fine.
No surprises, no ambiguity.

No upgrade needed.

Is your understanding of Jesus continuing to expand and deepen? How do you see Jesus differently than a decade ago, five years ago, a year ago? Do you tend to view Jesus as fully man or fully God? Consider holding these twin realities in one hand, being open to the transcendent Jesus (see Revelation 1:9-20) as well as the Jesus who made His home among us, within us.

You Have Heard It Said

(Matthew 5:33)

My literal friend,
so certain, so smug,
your truth set in stone,
scripture held prisoner
to a time long gone.

My literal friend,
release the shackles of time
and free God's eternal word.
Let it soar into our now,
breathing beauty and power
into the present,
dancing to the tune of new truths,
singing new verses
to songs written in ancient past,
for this time, this day,
this person.

My literal friend,
embrace story and symbol,
entertain metaphor and hyperbole,
open to poetic expression,
engage your imagination,
escape from the comfortable
shelter of the familiar,
awake from smug assuredness
exhibited by the Pharisees.

Free God to speak today.

What feelings arise as you read this reflection? Are you resistant? What is your view of scripture and how God communicates to you today? What might it look like for you to open to God and scripture in ways that free God to speak to you today—to enter into a real-time relationship with God who lives within you, surrounds you and interacts with you in real time?

BUT I SAY TO YOU

(MATTHEW 5:20)

Jesus shaking people from complacency,
shattering the once cozy confines of the commandments.
People who have cultivated a self-righteousness, a self-sufficiency
that leads from God, externally focused, burdensome.
Laws promoting individual fortitude and resolve,
papering over sins of the heart, helping to construct
a facade of righteousness, concealing hard, calloused hearts,
masking internal rebellion with external compliance.

With Jesus' "you have heard it said but I say to you,
your righteousness must exceed the righteousness of the Pharisees"
he grabs us by the heart, urging us
to pay attention to anger not murder,
lust not adultery, turning-the-other-cheek,
all-encompassing, non-retaliatory love—
personal integrity, not letter-of-the-law obedience,
emphasizing inner motivation and intention.

Jesus, a curator of hearts,
moving us from external requirements
that can be enforced, punished, measured, rewarded,
toward dependence on God,
internal God-stimulated transformation,
changing of heart and mind,
leading to wholehearted love of God,
self-sacrificially loving others.

How do you imagine the hearers reacted to these particular words of Jesus, to the comparisons that moved them inward, changed the focus from actions to internal desires and intentions? Reflecting on your own life, do you tend to focus on outward behaviors or pay attention to the issues of your heart? Ask God to reveal to you any current heart issue that invites further exploration. If something surfaces, give thanks for the wonderful gift of awareness.

COUNTING THE COST

(LUKE 14:25-33, 9:57-62)

As Jesus' clarion call
"follow me" is heard,
this invitation implies
a pause to count the cost,
time to consider,
to ponder the worthiness of
the One who asks.

Jesus calls it like it is—
No confusion, no bait-and-switch,
Jesus bids a person
to come and die.
The Via Dolorosa
is no yellow brick road.

Yes to Jesus means no to self,
a daily cross, losing one's life.
Yes, count the cost!
But once you've decided,
no excuses, don't look back.

What cost is attached to your call to follow Jesus? What are you unwilling to give up? Can you identify a desire or behavior that prevents you from more fully following? Could Jesus be asking more of you, in order to follow Jesus more closely? Please remember, this is about awareness, not condemnation, and awareness is the beginning of transformation.

THEY COME

(MATTHEW 4:23-25)

They come from cities and towns:
hungry, thirsty, desperate,
imprisoned, marginalized, despised.

They come, the tender shoots of hope
poking through the soil of their hearts,
fed by the stories they have heard,
praying they are true.

They come with fragile I-believe-
help-me-in-my-unbelief faith
and bold just-say-the-word faith.

They come
bringing friends, seeking healing.

They come for a touch,
for deliverance, sight, food.

They come
endeavoring to entrap, falsely accuse, kill.

They come to anoint,
to minister to, to be with.

They come to meet Jesus—
compassionate and powerful
full of grace and truth,
God's in-the-flesh love.

And they are seen, truly seen,
their hearts naked and exposed,
seen beyond and beneath their social standing,
gender, sexuality, station in life,
physical or spiritual malady.

How would you describe your faith? Imagine yourself coming to Jesus. Why do you come? Are you seeking love, grace, truth, forgiveness, healing? What do you desire from Jesus in this moment, this day, this season of life?

The Sabbath

(Mark 2:27-28, 3:4; Matthew 12:9-14; John 9:16)

A gift passed down for generations,
woven into the fabric of creation,
yet unwanted, unopened, deformed by
time and tradition—now unrecognizable,
a grotesque monstrosity.

A burdensome tool of oppression,
pompously guarded and defended,
a gatekeeper practice defining
who is in and who is out.
Sabbath breakers are definitely out,
grouped with sinners, tax gatherers,
prostitutes; all designated as
unrighteous, shunned by God.

Jesus, rightfully Lord of the Sabbath, and
knowing the Pharisees' hardened hearts,
takes on the position of Chief Sabbath Breaker,
blatantly and publicly breaks the rules,
choosing to heal again and again.
Surrounded by enemies trying to entrap him,
Jesus questions their motives and actions,
"Is it lawful to do good or evil,
save life or destroy it?"
The Pharisees remain silent.

The Sabbath made for people
not humans for the Sabbath—
a God-given gift of rest and refreshment!
The people rejoice
while the Pharisees plot
how to kill Jesus.

Do you see the Sabbath as a religious obligation or an invitation to greater health and wholeness? What keeps you from setting aside a day to be renewed and refreshed? List a few things that you already do or could do to bring yourself refreshment, and to try to enjoy God's gift of Sabbath on a regular basis.

SILENCE AND SOLITUDE

(LUKE 4:42)

Silence, solitude—
so strange, unfamiliar
even shunned
as loneliness, rejection.
We remain tethered
to treadmills of responsibility
screens, cell phones
smart watches
communication
information.

Yet
silence and solitude
are escorts to the universe
enabling discovery
unheard in the hustle
unknown in the hectic
the harried of hard-hearted
deadlines.

Yes
silence and solitude
offer unhurried space
foster an unhurried internal pace
which, in time,
may shape the external
rising and resting,
working and leisure.

In this spaciousness
we need not seek God
rather enter into
be opened to, given to

listening, hearing
seeing, being with
naked and unashamed
seen and loved
as we are
freed to love others
freed to be loved
beyond time and space
yet firmly in time and space
in God's loving grace.

Jesus sought time alone
in quiet spaces
to hear from the Father
reassuring words of love
strengthening, fortifying
identifying.
So too our hearts
need time alone
for strengthening, fortifying
softening.

How do you feel about silence, solitude? What, if anything, do you fear? Why do you think Jesus pulled away from the crowds, and even His disciples, to be alone with God? What comes up for you when you consider being alone, being silent? Do you sense God inviting you to explore one or both of these spiritual practices? If yes, what might be some first steps for you to take?

THE WEDDING HAIKU

(JOHN 2:1-11)

a mother's request,
God nods, Lucifer trembles,
water becomes wine.

Are you surprised that this is Jesus' first recorded miracle? Notice the inter-play between Mary, Jesus, God the Father and Satan. What does this miracle reveal about God's heart and involvement in the world? What is its message for you?

On the Mountain

(Matthew 5:3-12)

Scampering up the grassy hill we pause,
we look at each other,
pants wet from the droplets that hitched a ride on the climb.
"What are we doing?"

We are drawn to this man by...
curiosity? boredom? the stories circulating about him?
Miracle worker, rebel, guru, nutcase—
enough to get us out of bed and scurrying up this hillside,
and believe me, we are not the only ones.

His first words immediately draw us in
like water on a dry sponge, a morsel to a famished child.
"Blessed..."—a gentle breeze blowing within, a cold drink of water,
the first bite of a crisp apple—"Blessed are those who..."

But what follows those promising, hope-filled words?
nails on a chalkboard, teeth grinding in the night, unsettling!
That first crisp bite revealing half a worm.
Words generating immediate, perverse internal discord.

Those first promising words, "blessed are those,"
are followed by words of pain,
concepts that do not console.

Yet
I do not turn away.
He, His words, His presence, unsettling yet not.

I choose instead to loosen my grip on those first inviting words
and open to the unsettling—
poor in spirit, those who mourn,
the merciful and meek, hungry and thirsty,
pure, peacemakers, persecuted.

An invitation beneath what is heard, known,
an invitation into the messiness of life,
a blessedness forged in the crucible of counter-cultural living.

What draws you to Jesus? Take time to read through the Beatitudes (Matthew 5:3-12). As you read each description of the blessed ones, which do you find most difficult to embrace? Choose one to take with you today and recall it throughout your daily interactions. Reflect on it again this evening; where did God reveal blessedness in you or in others?

PERSECUTED, INSULTED, VILIFIED

(MATTHEW 5:10-12, JOHN 15:18-20)

came in love
came to serve
offering life
offering hope
teaching peace
unacknowledged
unreceived
conspired against
ridiculed
persecuted

Blessed are the persecuted
theirs, the kingdom of God —

attempts to stone him
determined to accuse him
drive him from the town
throw him off a cliff
seeking to entrap him
scheming to arrest him
spitting on him
striking him
beating him
mocking him

Great is your heavenly reward
counted among the prophets—

insulted, vilified
out of his mind
a sinner, a drunkard
demon-possessed
raving mad

impure spirit
not from God
blasphemer
Sabbath breaker
Samaritan

The world hated me first.
No servant is greater than their master.

What emotions does this poem elicit? How might someone consider persecution, insults, vilification a positive? In which of your life circumstances
do you find it most difficult to speak out about your faith, about the love and
justice of God? Share your struggles with God. How does knowing how Jesus
went through these struggles help you deal with the same type of experiences
in your own life?

Do Not Murder

(Matthew 5:21-22)

Murder, unimaginable!
But anger—
acceptable, justifiable,
even admirable.

Jesus shatters our complacency
undermines our smug certainty
by making anger and murder
synonymous—
unrighteous, sinful.

For anger cannot be contained.
It boils over, consumes, rages,
burns, devours, smolders;
ignites bitterness,
resentfulness,
hostility, hatred.

Anger lashes out, attacks,
wounds, harms, destroys;
is wrathful, vengeful;
provokes strife, dissension,
trouble, discord, conflict;
derails righteousness,
God's desire for peace.

So, be slow
to rage, fume, seethe,
fly off the handle,
blow a gasket,
have a fit, hit the roof,
flip your lid, wig out,
see red.

Deal with your anger
before bitterness takes root
and grows,
hot spots flair, flames destroy.

What role does anger play in your life? What are the types of circumstances that tend to lead to an eruption of anger? Spend some time unpacking those types of circumstances, seeking to identify the underlining issues. Share what you discover with God.

OUR

(MATTHEW 6:5-13, JOHN 17:20-21, *CF.* EPHESIANS 3:17-19)

Oh God, rescue me
from my self-centered,
tightly structured
Jesus-and-me world.

Expand my heart,
enlarge my vision,
help me to embrace
the our-ness inherent
in the love of God.

Deliver me from
myopic prayer—
my Father, my will,
my daily bread.
Help me to see the world not as mine,
not yours, not hers, not his…

Ours.
Our Father
Our daily bread
Our trespasses
Our forgiveness and forgiving
Lead *us,* deliver *us* from temptation and evil.

Extricate from me
selfish, status quo acceptance,
thoughts and acts that
isolate and insulate and
prevent me from growing
love for God and neighbor.

For only *together,*
with my sisters and brothers,

can I begin to know and accept
the extravagant dimensions
of the Love of Christ.

Open my heart to the "our" and "us"
of living Jesus undivided,
for unity, oneness, our-ness, us-ness
declares to our world in need,
demonstrates to our world in deed,
the inclusive love of Christ.

As you pray the Lord's prayer, who is and who is not in your *our*? What are your feelings and thoughts around the phrase *inclusive love of Christ*? In which areas is God inviting you to grow regarding your ability to love, embrace, accept others? How can you begin to act on God's invitation?

FASTING

Losing sight of Jesus
   the bread of life
   the living water
I focus on
   not eating
   denial of self
I begin to sink
beneath the relentless waves
of hunger
drowning in the sea
of self-indulgence
unable to cry out for help
my mouth
stuffed with food.

What experience do you have with fasting? Is your focus on your hunger or your presence with Jesus? Ask God to be with you as you fast from food or other indulgences and use your hunger pangs as a springboard to prayer.

LET GO OF

(MATTHEW 6:19-21; JOHN 5:44, 12:43)

rust-destroying
moth-eating
thief-stealing
temporal treasures—

glory-lusting
praise-seeking
people-pleasing
making-others-happy
encounters—

false humility
value-denying
beggar-bowl-carrying
fill-me-up
make-me-feel-significant
transactions—

fear-fueled
anxiety-laden
scarcity-saturated
striving—

escapist
head-in-the-sand
spiritualizing
rapture-loving
wind-and-wave-denying
mindset.

Fix your eyes on Jesus
Set your mind on Christ
Open your heart, ears, eyes
to the words, works of God—

the now and coming of
God's kingdom, God's will,
God's love in transformational fullness.

Where your treasure, your focus, is
so shall your heart be.

Which temporal treasures do you most desire? What do they provide for you? Take time to explore the level of your heart's desire for God, God's will, God's kingdom. How might you find what you are desiring from treasures in God? What are some spiritual practices that might help you change your focus?

JESUS THE CONTRARIAN

(LUKE 6:27-36)

Insanity!
the message of Jesus
falls on deaf ears in the
what's-in-it-for-me,
stand-up-for-yourself,
protect-what's-yours world.

"Love your enemies"
What about…?

"Pray for those who mistreat you"
Does that mean…?

"Turn the other cheek"
Even if…?!

"Give to those in need"
Everyone?

Unlike Mary, who sought clarity—
"How can this be?"
—we look for loopholes, limits,
explanations, justification,
crying out with the Pharisees,
"Who is my neighbor?"

"Be merciful as your Father is merciful,"
Jesus' uncompromising response.

Which of the above words of Jesus are a challenge for you? To which do you feel most drawn? How does being merciful to others invite you into the heart of God? Seek to be aware of how you experience the mercy of God in your life today and where you extend it to others.

TAKE A WALK WITH JESUS

Although we understand walking alone is often an opportunity to pray, we may not realize that a walk in itself can become prayer. Here's how:

- Walk slowly and deliberately, using all of your five senses as you go.
- Notice how your body moves, how it supports you, how much energy is expended in order to walk. In this moment, how do you feel? Do you have pain? Do you feel pleasure? Does the exercise feel tedious or tiring?
- Notice the light, the warmth of the sun, the air on your skin, the colors surrounding you.
- Begin to notice greater detail in patterns, shapes, textures around you, the shades and contrasts of color, in the juxtapositions and relations of the things in your surroundings.
- Touch and feel. Pick up stones, twigs, earth, leaves and hold them gently.
- Try to stop thinking and simply be. Let everything drop away; try to be totally present to your sensations.
- Begin to notice smells more acutely, the scent of growing things, of the earth itself.
- Listen to the range of sounds, far-off distant sounds, immediate or close sounds, even your own breathing.
- You may want to keep a memento from your walk, something you particularly enjoyed or that holds meaning for you.
- You may wish to end your walk by journaling, consciously noting what feelings and thoughts came to you during your prayer walk. Perhaps you want to end with a thanksgiving exercise, specifically listing gifts God offered you during your walk.

PRIESTLY SPRINKLER

(MATTHEW 5:45)

The whirly-bird sprinkler stands
in the center of the yard
like a priest before her congregation.
Head revolving side-to-side
spraying all in her path
her relentless tck-tck-tck-tck
returning and repeating the ritual
again and again and again.

This priestly sprinkler spraying
blessing, forgiveness, liquid love,
on the beautifully dressed roses,
the seasonal golden poppies,
simple daisies, purple lavender, even the
we-do-not-want-you-here weeds.

This priestly sprinkler has no religious rules
limiting who can be blessed and forgiven,
the tck-tck-tck-tck love spray is for all,
indiscriminate, unconditional—
birds, rabbits, skunks, even rats
show up for early morning blessings,
while hummingbirds frequent
the early evening services
darting here and there,
glistening in the setting sun.

Mid-summer services
bring swimsuit-clad children,
irreverent and rambunctious,
unable to stand still.
Undaunted, the whirly-bird sprinkler priest
continues spraying tck-tck-tck-tck

blessings, forgiveness flowing freely,
bathing, baptizing, drenching them
in abundant liquid love.

What do these lines communicate about God's love, forgiveness and blessings? Do you agree with the indiscriminate nature of God as a priestly sprinkler? Ask God to expand your heart to love, forgive and bless others. What do you desire to experience from God today? Ask God to help you notice God and God's love in the ordinary and daily things of life.

You Have Your Reward

(Matthew 6:1-4, 6:14-16)

Proud peacocks
displaying their pharisaic plumage,
strutting roosters
with their pompous religiosity,
spotlight-grabbing actors
seeking fame,
pursuing personal praise,
attention-seeking do-gooders,
trumpet-blasting charity givers,
loudmouthed pious prayers,
flamboyant fasters:
all acts seeking admiration
and glory from others.
You have your reward.

Are you overly concerned about the opinions of those around you? To whom do you look for self-worth, significance and belonging: God or others? From whom do you desire praise and recognition? This week, practice the discipline of secret service, showing love in tangible ways that do not readily identify you. Pay attention to how it feels to love without receiving thanks or praise.

When I Pray

(Matthew 6:6)

When I pray, I do not feel your presence,
    yet I know you are here, forever faithful.

When I pray, I do not feel your tender embrace,
    yet I know you are here, wrapped all around me.

When I pray, I do not feel your soothing love,
    yet I know you are here, loving me in this moment and the next,
    and the next and the next.

When I pray, I know beyond words, beyond feelings, you are here—
    caring for me,
    listening to me,
    embracing me,
    and that is enough for me (at least for now).

Do you feel God's presence when you pray? To whom do you pray (Father, God, Jesus, Holy Spirit)? When God feels distant, when your prayers seem to bounce off the ceiling, how do you react? Turn your attention right now toward God; open your heart—asking, listening, sharing, praying.

EYES AND EARS

(MARK 8:18)

Eyes easily drawn to glittery images,
things fleeting, temporal;
ears inclined to flattery, praise,
words that puff up, convey importance.

Our eyes, our ears, so readily betray us.
Blind to what we refuse to see,
deaf to what we choose to ignore
or cannot hear—
ideas that threaten our complacency,
our thinking, our values, our worldview.
Blind, deaf, to new invitations and
challenges of Jesus.

God, give me a listening, seeing heart—
heart-ears that hear the Spirit's voice,
heart-eyes that see what the Father is doing—
a heart that beats in rhythm with Your heart.

What draws your attention away from the kingdom of God? Whose voice is more compelling than the call of God on your life? What does it look like to cooperate with the Holy Spirit in cultivating a listening, seeing heart, or ears to hear His voice and eyes to see what God has done or is doing? Consider making the last stanza of this poem your prayer for the next week.

Judging Others

(Luke 6:37, Matthew 7:1-6)

When pointing my accusing finger,
three fingers point back at me.
My hand designed by God
to remind me of the seriousness
of judging—
for when I judge I too am judged.

These three fingers pointing back
caution me to not judge quickly, rashly,
maybe not at all and
perhaps instead a prompt to
look three times inside myself,
asking God for eyes to see my brokenness,
my shortcomings, my hurtful ways,
to name and own the log in my own eye.

Next time instead of thrusting an accusing finger,
I will reach out my hand in graciousness, kindness,
extending the mercy I deeply desire God to give to me.

Why do you think it can be so easy to go to judgment? Are you one who tends to judge quickly or extend grace? Are you inclined to be suspicious or easily able to give the benefit of the doubt? Spend time contemplating your brokenness, asking God to reveal to you the logs in your own eye, and then spend time soaking in God's love and forgiveness of you.

NOT WHAT IT SEEMS

(MATTHEW 7:9-11)

These circumstances
this news
this hurt
this struggle
this cancer
this failed marriage
this job loss, house loss
this devastating death
this car wreck of a life.

For this I am to be thankful?
This I am to receive as a gift from God?

NO.

This reality is not as it should be,
as God designed.
Tattered rags of reality the norm,
adversity flowing freely
in a broken, sin-drenched world
experiences that eclipse,
obscure, conceal God's gifts
God's goodness
God's grace, love, presence.

God's sustaining gifts of fish and loaves
appear as snakes and stones
tattered-rag reality—undermining
faith in God's faithful provision.

As you look at the current realities of your life, do you see snakes and stones or fish and loaves? What are the places you wrestle with God's goodness and love, and with the truth that God is in control, all-powerful? What does your current experience affirm for you about the person of God? How are your feelings and your circumstances affecting your relationship with God? Ask God to help you see or sense the reality of goodness, grace and provision that you are not able to recognize: the sprouts of grace, the tendrils of love that are also present.

FRUIT TREES

(MATTHEW 7:16-19, JOHN 15:1-2)

God's tree planted deep within
the relational soil of faith,
sustained by the Spirit, watered,
bathed by streams of living waters,
tried, tested, pruned, nurtured,
strengthened by circumstances,
soil cultivated by Gardener God.

This tree bearing a single fruit,
which, like a tangerine, is comprised of
individual wedges, nine to be exact—
love, joy, peace, patience, kindness,
goodness, faithfulness, gentleness,
self-control—and like a tangerine
this fruit is contained within a thin membrane
accessible only when
the protective membrane is torn.

Only when the protection is penetrated
can the fruit be tasted,
its aroma and texture experienced,
only then its fruit revealed.
A tantalizing tangerine can hang
in the morning sun, an inviting orange orb
that promises sweetness,
but is without scent or flavor—
the orange orb containing vile substance,
foul, unfit to eat.

What fruit does your life yield when torn, jostled, bumped by circumstances? Sometimes the fruit is sweet, but other times tasteless, withered, unavailable. Remember a few such occasions—the surrounding circumstances, people involved, your spiritual, physical and emotional state at the time. Such reflection leads to awareness, enabling us to be ready, be "prayed up," for life challenges.

Now look at the nine wedges of the fruit of the Spirit (love, joy, peace, patience, kindness, goodness, faithfulness, gentleness, self-control). Which do you feel comes easily; which is a struggle? And most importantly, which is God inviting you to intentionally cultivate with God's guidance and support?

DOING FOR JESUS

(MATTHEW 7:21-23)

Making God in our own image,
we convince ourselves
of the importance
of producing for the kingdom,
doing for God.

We commit to serving—
Sunday school, soup kitchens,
short term mission trips;
writing checks, moving mountains,
making miracles, driving out demons,
prophesying, throwing ourselves into
acts deemed worthy of doing.

Never do we think to ask
what God desires.
Is it because God's response
would be to embrace our first love?
How very unproductive.
Is it because we want to do
what we want to do?
No denial of self,
no daily taking up the cross,
but following God as we choose.

To His energetic, doing followers,
having recited their laundry lists
of good and noble Christian deeds,
approved of and applauded
by their peers,
Jesus has some shocking
and sobering words,

"I never knew you.
Away from Me, you evildoers!"

What warning does this reflection communicate? Why is it important that our doing for God be an outflow of being with God? What might God say to you about your life, and what success is and is not? What are the daily, weekly, or yearly practices that help your life flow from being with God? What practices might you add or remove that would help you to spend time being with God?

Be Ready

(Luke 6:46-49)

A storm is coming.
No escaping,
but we can prepare,
build a firm foundation,
fix and fasten shutters
fortify, endure, prevail.

No deliverance,
no avoidance
(in this world you WILL HAVE tribulation)
but you will not weather it alone—
There is One who will be with you in it.

Now is the time to combine the sand
of relational obedience with the
outpouring of living waters—
the concrete mix of God's word
—knowing God's presence, God's peace
(a peace in spite of not because of)
to avoid being swept away
by the torrents of destruction.

Our ability, our courage to stand strong,
a byproduct of relational connection
with the One who quiets the storm,
the One who overcomes the final storm
racing toward each of us—death.

How do you rate your relational obedience to God? In which circumstances do you find it most difficult to trust God, sense God's presence, know God's peace, depend on God's word? Does knowing God is with you in difficult times help you, as you journey through them? How might you partner with God in deepening your trust of God?

KEYS TO THE GOOD LIFE

(MATTHEW 5:3-12)

A new purveyor of prosperous
and privileged living has come
to town touting his teaching re:
living an abounding, abundant,
booming, blooming, blossoming life.

This is no get-rich-quick scheme
no pathway to instant success
but a redefining, reorienting, a kind of you-have-
heard-it-said-but-I-say-to-you message…

Contrary, conflicting, contradictory,
divergent, different to the point of being
antagonistic, hostile, to previous purveyors
of the good life, to one's own soul
a message unnerving, even intimidating—

The pursuit of riches, opulence, affluence replaced
by the need to admit one's personal poverty

Seeking of happiness and joy exchanged
for mourning

The desire to be in control, powerful, dominate
swapped out for meekness

The **quest to satisfy, gratify, indulge**
put aside for hungering and thirsting for righteousness

The **killer instinct, take-no-prisoners mentality**
becomes a call to be merciful

Pragmatism gives way to pursuing purity of heart

Peace-keeping, placating, people-pleasing exchanged
with peacemaking, courageously speaking love-inspired truth

Longing for praise, admiration, appreciation, applause,
becoming a willingness to be persecuted, insulted,
blamed, falsely accused,

Long-held ways of looking at, thinking about life,
turned inside out, upside down,
a different life from a different source—
a God-life.

What does this reflection convey about the person and values of Jesus? Which of the characteristics above is most compelling to you? Which is most challenging? Which attitudes or perspectives is God inviting you to embrace more fully? Ask Jesus to help you become less of the person described in bold letters above and more of who God has created and called you to be.

NICK AT NIGHT

(JOHN 3:1-9)

Timidly, under the cover of darkness,
he comes seeking the Light that is life.
Cautiously he approaches, much to lose,
but something urges him on,
an inner knowing—this man is different
sent from God, partnering with God, maybe more
—but he dares not let his heart go there,
not yet.

Rabbi, teach me.
Jesus responds with nonsense.

Must be born again,
kingdom of God,
water and Spirit,
the wind blowing where it will…
his head is spinning
as he mumbles to Jesus, to himself
how is this possible?

But his heart is strangely engaged,
his spirit quickened, the wind is blowing.
For the Light is beginning to overcome
the darkness of his intellect,
the fortress of his well-established creed.
Unimaginable truth being planted within,
changing Nicodemus,
changing everything!

How has the truth of the gospel changed your life? How is your perspective on life, God, others, your circumstances different after being born again? How are Jesus and His teaching changing you? What are the truths of the gospel that you recall to heart and mind that form and shape your thinking, interactions with others, the person you are?

MORE LOVE
(JOHN 3:16)

we are powerless
to make
God love us
less

or

love us
more

for
infinite love
loves infinitely

How is God's infinite love for you informing and shaping your sense of self (beloved of God), sense of God (your lover)? What does the knowledge that God loves loving you stir within you? Share your thoughts and questions with God. Seek to be mindful regarding this truth about God's infinite love for you, paying attention to how it has an impact on your sense of self and your interactions with others.

Jesus' Plain Truth

(John 3:10-21)

Listen carefully! I am speaking truth—
sharing what I have lived,
seen with my own eyes,
no secondhand insights, no hearsay.

Yet you turn from my testimony,
refusing my truth, me,
using rational objections,
intellectual questions,
to distance me far from your hungry heart.

I offer you freedom, forgiveness,
belonging, love, grace,
assurance of full and lasting life—
not pointing an accusing finger but
opening wide my arms, begging you to come.

Yet you turn from love, from me, run to darkness—
addicted to denial, fearing exposure, trapped in illusion.
I stand waiting, arms open wide,
imploring you to come,
to know freedom, eternal life.

What is Jesus/God revealing to you that you may not be willing to receive? What fears, addictions, illusions, hinder your ability to have ears to hear and eyes to see? Pray to more fully embrace the freedom, forgiveness, belonging, love, grace, assurance of a full and lasting life with God. What new areas of freedom may God be inviting you to enter into?

Blow, Wind, Blow

(John 3:5-8)

Blow, wind, blow,
renew, refresh our spirits,
our hearts, our souls.

Blow, wind, blow,
carry us away into your love
into a deep knowing,
of who, whose we are.

Blow, wind, blow,
lift us high into yourself,
that we may see as you see,
sense your essence in others.

Blow, wind, blow,
clear away the pollution in our minds,
judgments, anxiety,
the tumbleweeds of complacency.

Blow, wind, blow,
shake the dust from theological foundations,
free us from attachments that shackle,
fan the fresh air of rebirth.

Blow, wind, blow,
let us feel the gale within us,
the exhilaration of your free-flowing love,
inspiration, invitation to create, to become.

Blow, wind, blow,
gliding on currents of the Spirit,
kites soaring, dancing before you,
vital manifestations of your power and presence.

Which of the above stanzas best expresses your current desires regarding your God-life? Which of the verses do you sense God inviting/challenging you to embrace? What might that look like?

BUBBLES

(JOHN 3:8, MATTHEW 11:28-30 (THE MESSAGE))

perfect spheres
effortlessly floating
large and small
some ascending
some descending

ALL carried upon the breeze
fragile
fleeting
beautiful
(not one the master of their own destiny)

each an ethereal invitation-challenge
to live differently
uninhibited
to let go of striving
to be

embracing the unforced rhythms
of God's grace
God's Spirit guiding
God's love sustaining
freely living

I dip my wand
in the soapy solution
and breathing deeply pray
I may float freely
on the wind of God's Spirit.

The above phrase "unforced rhythms of God's grace" is a very slight rewording of a phrase from Eugene Peterson's
The Message (MSG), Matthew 11:28-30.

What feelings arise as you read some of the phrases above—unforced rhythms of grace, freely living, Spirit guiding, love sustaining? When in your life do you feel freedom to be "bubbles on the breath of God," to float effortlessly, follow the wind of God's Spirit, or just be? What is God's invitation to you through this reflection? What keeps you from living freely and lightly, embracing the unforced rhythms of God's grace? Ask God to help you to float a little more freely on the wind of the Spirit.

The above phrase, "unforced rhythms of grace," is a quotation from Eugene Peterson's *The Message (MSG)*, Matthew 11:28-30.

BLOWING BUBBLES
(YOU WILL NEED TO PURCHASE BUBBLE SOLUTION.)

This exercise is a reminder that God, our Creator, calls us to be in harmony with the winds of God's Spirit in our lives.

As you blow the bubbles, imagine the breath of God creating those bubbles. Imagine you are one of those bubbles, and God is breathing life into you. The wand is Christ, reminding you that all things were made in and through Him.

Use a lot of breath or a little, noticing the difference. Are you able to direct the bubbles where you want them to go? Pay attention to your bubbles, watching them float and dance, and experiment on the currents of the wind. Reflect on the words "unforced rhythms of grace," taken from Matthew 11:28-30 (MSG). What would it mean for you to be God's bubble, floating upon the unforced currents of God's grace, allowing God complete control over your direction and duration? Share your feelings and thoughts with God.

The Actors

(Matthew 6:1-4, 6:14-16)

Honor seeking,
Yearning for personal prominence,
Pious pretenders proudly performing and
Openly pursuing positions of distinction—
Craving praise,
Recognition and respect—
Illuminating their devout deeds,
Thirsty for attention, standing and status,
Esteem-starved actors clamoring for the
Spotlight of religion's center stage.

As you live a life of faith, do you find yourself concerned about the opinions of others? To whom do you look for a sense of value, significance and belonging—God or others? Why is approval important to you? How might owning who you are in Christ—a new creation, God's masterpiece—release you from the internal desire/need for the approval of others?

WOMAN AT THE WELL

(JOHN 4:1-26)

I approached the well
at my usual time, middle of the day,
the sun baking the dry earth;
no one is ever around.

I know I've made a mess of my life,
bad choice after bad choice,
no one needs to remind me.

In the heat of midday
no waggling tongues,
no accusing fingers,
no averted eyes.

But today was different—
A man was at the well,
a Jew no less,
a self-righteous,
I-am-better-than-you Jew,
or so I thought.

As I approached the well,
he spoke to me,
he, a Jew,
I, a Samaritan woman;
if only he knew with whom he was speaking.

He asked for a drink,
but I was the one who left refreshed,
forever changed.

I look forward to collecting my water tomorrow
in the cool of the morning
new and known.

Reflect on who you are now that you have tasted Jesus' living water. How has your encounter with Jesus changed you? Are you able to own and embrace the wonder of who you are—no longer defined by your past, but defined by God, transformed by love? Spend some time reflecting on the wonder of who you are as God's new creation.

I AM/I WAS/I AM

(JOHN 3:3)

I ~~am~~ was a sinner, dead in trespasses and sin
I ~~am~~ was a leper, naked and blind
I ~~am~~ was an enemy of God
I ~~am~~ was on the outside looking in.

I am now and forever
a beloved child of God
forgiven
adopted
chosen
justified and sanctified.

I am now and forever
a new creation
a masterpiece
free to receive love
free to freely love
free to be, to become.

I am now and forever
known
loved
cherished
enjoyed
by the Triune God.

The above poem speaks of our unshakable identity as articulated in the scriptures: who we are because of Jesus' life, death and resurrection. Consider the wonder of being re-created in and through Christ. Who is God inviting you to let go of within yourself, and who is God inviting you to own more of? Which descriptors are you drawn to? Which are more difficult for you to embrace? Choose one and carry it with you today, allowing it to remind you of who you are and whose you are.

SPRINGS OF LIVING WATER

(JOHN 4:14, 7:38)

This gentle Spring
is also a river within
flowing water bringing
refreshment, renewal,
replenishment, life.

Yet not merely a babbling brook
an unassuming trickle of water
easily dismissed, effortlessly ignored
this is a flowing river bringing change—

for water is a force,
a transformative power,
hollowing out mountains,
converting granite cliff to sandy beaches,
carving out canyons.

Jesus is not offering a sip,
a stream to soak feet in on
a hot day—but a river that
will change us, mold us,
shape us—refining, sculpting
the landscape of our hearts.

Crafting us into a tributary
bringing refreshment, renewal,
replenishment, life, ushering in
change, refining, sculpting
the landscape of others' hearts.

How are you currently experiencing or not experiencing the living water that is Jesus? How has your heart been changed? Where do you see springs of living water wanting to come forth in your life? How are you making space for this or where are you blocking the way? How are you being this transformative presence in the lives of others?

NOT MY PIGS!

(MATTHEW 8:28-34)

I like Jesus the healer, miracle-worker,
rebel, Sabbath-breaker,
anti-religious-establishment resister,
the woman-affirming, empowering defender,
friend of the marginalized.

But not the pig-drowning,
serve-one-master,
sell-all-you-have,
turn the other cheek,
bless-those-who-curse-you,
pick-up-your-cross,
seek-first-the-kingdom
Jesus.

When Jesus starts eyeing my stuff—
portfolio, property, home(s),
retirement account, car, hobbies—
all I count mine,
I begin to get uneasy.

I want him to move on.
Stick it to those in power,
perform a miracle for some down-and-outer,
someone who truly needs what Jesus offers.

Never realizing the healing,
the freedom he offers.
Unable, unwilling
to own my own need.
I send him on his way
and head off to Church.

What is it about the teaching of Jesus that makes you a bit uneasy? When you imagine Jesus eyeing your stuff—portfolio, property, home(s), toys, collections, retirement account, car, hobbies—do you feel a little discomfort? Have there been times when you have desired to send Jesus away? Share all this with Jesus.

FOUR SOILS, ONE HEART

(LUKE 8:4-15)

Jesus sowing the seeds of God's word
casting them on the soil of my heart
disclosing, revealing
an uneven topography within me
a variety of seeds
strewn over patchy ground.

"Blessed be..." seeds
"But I say to you..." seeds
"Seventy times seven..." seeds
Self-sacrificial seeds
"Follow me..." seeds
"Our Father..." seeds
"Love your enemy..." seeds
"Seek first the kingdom..." seeds
"Treasure in heaven..." seeds
"Love God, love others..." seeds
"Do not judge..." seeds
"Turn the other cheek..." seeds
"First shall be last..." seeds
"Love one another..." seeds
"Fear not..." seeds
"Better that I leave..." seeds
"Greater things than these..." seeds
Sabbath seeds
Servant seeds
Cross-bearing seeds
Grace seeds
Childlike seeds
Disciple-making seeds
Truth seeds

Jesus freely scatters over
the fertile, tilled meadows and
dry barren fields
of my heart—

Soil one
Seeds landing on the hard path of disappointment
trampled down by hurts too agonizing to name
gobbled up by birds of despair
producing no roots.

Soil two
Seeds landing on hopeful soil of superficial acceptance
but without depth and moisture
faltering in harsh circumstances
withering in the scorching sun.

Soil three
Seeds landing on promising, but untended soil
sprouting, taking root
only to be choked out by weeds of worry,
or the deceitfulness of riches.

Soil four
Seeds landing on fertile, cultivated soil
receptive, welcoming, nurturing,
sprouting, flourishing, yielding a crop,
thirty, sixty, a hundredfold.

Jesus sowing the seeds of God's word
casting them on the soil of my heart
disclosing, revealing
the uneven topography within me.

Keeping in mind the four types of soil, read through the list of seeds listed above. Consider the level of receptivity in your heart and put the corresponding soil number next to each seed listed. Honestly reflect—what is your resistance to those to which you gave a one? Ask God to heal your pain and soften your heart. What is attractive about the seeds to which you assigned a two? What keeps these from taking root? Take a hard look at the threes. What are your concerns, the distractions that hinder these seeds from maturing and producing lasting fruit? What may God be inviting you to weed out of your life? Finally, celebrate your fours, gratefully acknowledging the growth and fruitfulness in your life and the lives of others; ask God to reveal any weeds that may threaten your flourishing.

STOP, LOOK AND LISTEN

Take some time to go back and review your journal entries since you began Section Two, using one or more of the prompts below. You may want to do this over a few days.

WORD/PHRASE

Write out the words/phrases/questions that stood out to you in the previous reflections, thoughts that drew you in or caused resistance, affected you positively or negatively, moved you in some way. Try using different colored pens to represent different emotions. Pay attention to and make note of your feelings, listening attentively for the invitations or challenges God gives you.

EXPLORING THEMES

Attempt to discover what message(s) God has for you. What might God be inviting or challenging you to embrace, live into? If a particular theme surfaces, consider the nature of it. Is it more of an invitation (something you long for and welcome) or a challenge (something to overcome)?

What do you notice about Jesus through these poems and questions? Does anything surprise you? How might your feelings toward or your experience of Jesus be shifting, expanding, deepening?

NEVER MADE IT EASY

(LUKE 9:57-61)

Come follow me

Before I could answer

But count the cost
Deny self
Pick up cross
No place to lay head
Sell all
Let dead bury dead
No time for goodbyes
Hate mother, father.

Then

Are you coming?

How are you responding to Jesus' invitation to follow, in light of the costs attached? Which of the costs mentioned cause you to hesitate? What might Jesus be asking of you today?

THE TOUCH

(MARK 5:24-34)

desperate, unseen
pushing through the crowd
years of disappointment
thousands wasted
nothing to lose.

she has heard the tales (who hasn't)
but she is a woman
no standing in the culture
why would he help her?

she eyes him up ahead
her pace and heart quicken
unnoticed, she moves closer
now within reach

hoping against hope
longing for a miracle
she stretches out her hand
touches his cloak.

in that moment
(she knows her body)
she feels different
stops
she is healed
disappears into the crowd
joyous!

a voice rings out
"who touched me?"
he knows.

fearfully she moves toward him
the crowd parting before her
trembling, she kneels
awaiting the familiar words
reproach, reprimand, rebuke
words that rekindle her shame.

lifting her to her feet
looking into her eyes
he speaks
words that reach deeper
than her healing.

"daughter"

she is different
(she knows her spirit)
suddenly alive, whole
seen, known.

"be free in body, soul, spirit"

she stands to her full height
(healed body, soul, spirit).

"your faith has made you well"

cured, empowered
she walks away
seen, known
whole.

How is the woman different after her encounter with Jesus? What gift does Jesus give her beyond healing? Notice Jesus' posture and intentionality toward her—how are you like this woman? Share your desires openly with Jesus.

GENEROSITY OF GOD

(LUKE 8:39)

"...tell how much God has done for you."

No stingy, tightfisted God here.
No dribbling of resources, piecemeal handouts,
scarcity thinking, miserly polices,
bean-counting practices,
grudgingly given tin trinkets.

Abundance, lavishness, extravagance,
magnanimousness, wastefulness;
excessive, overflowing, brimming,
boundary-bursting, mind-boggling generosity
freely flowing from God to us.

Water becomes wine—really good wine
—sun rises and rain falls on all,
fish and loaves feeding thousands,
living springs gushing water,
quenching thirsty souls,
with abundant grace and truth.

Nothing, God withholds nothing.
God's one and only son
willingly, lovingly given,
grace gushing from pierced hands,
feet and side.
Nothing, not even Jesus.

When has God surprised you with His love, abundance? Where are you currently experiencing God's abundance? Which of the gospel stories is most meaningful to you when considering God's lavish, abundant love? How can your acknowledgement of God's generosity help you more generously serve others?

I WONDER

(JOHN 5:41, 5:44, 7:18, 12:43)

What if I didn't care, I mean really didn't care about what people said or thought about me?

What if my identity, sense of worth, belonging and significance were all grounded in the actions and words of Jesus?

What if I truly believed, with total certainty, that God loves me, delights in me, even likes and enjoys me, and that love will never change?

Would I live differently? Would I live Jesus more fully?

Would I feel free to be the one-of-a-kind masterpiece God created me to be?

Would I feel free to own all that I am—my quirks, brokenness, gifts, abilities and struggles—without pride or hiding or condemnation?

Would I claim the assurance flowing from my deep belief that nothing can separate me from the unconditional love of God?

What if I believed, really believed, God is for me and not against me; that I am truly a child of God; that God is actively loving me into this moment and the next, not out of some self-imposed divine duty, but because God loves loving me?

Would I be more willing to love others—the marginalized, my enemies? Would I return blessing for cursing, love without strings attached?

I wonder.

How do you think God sees you? How might you begin to fully embrace the truth of who you are as God's creation, child, beloved? How does it feel to identify yourself as His beloved; is it a struggle or is it easy? What hinders you from believing God's commitment to be with you, to love you with a nothing-can-separate-you-from-God love? How might owning these truths affect your ability to love and serve others, to follow fully and freely as God leads?

NOT SHARING MY STORY

My life filled to overflowing
My emails screaming for a reply
My calendar controlling my every move
My pain, my sorrow, my struggles silenced
My heart ignored, not shared
My story untold, even to You.

Why?!

Why do I binge watch?
Why do I pour that extra glass of wine?
Why do lose myself in hobbies?
Why do I keep myself to myself
choosing to numb me to me
and even to You.

Why?!

I believe in You—Your love, Your closeness
Your for-me-ness, Your grace and mercy
Your care and compassion
Your listening ear
Your involvement in this world,
in my life.

Why?!

Why do I not share my story—my struggles,
my joys, my triumphs, my despair with You?
Why do I not open my heart, my soul to You?
Why do I busy myself with meaningless activity,
with anything that gets in the way of speaking to You?
listening to You?
Why do I live contrary to what I say I believe?

Why?!

When You say I can ask for what I want
that I can share freely and honestly
that You will give me the desires of my heart,
when You remind me that nothing can separate me from Your love,
why don't I share my heart with You?

Do I really believe You?
Do I truly trust You?
Do I have confidence in the truths
demonstrated by the cross and the resurrection?
embodied in a piece of bread and a cup of wine?

I do believe
help me in my unbelief.
Make Your presence known to me
help me to have seeing eyes and listening ears
an attentive heart.
Help me be willing to be known by You,
to share my unfolding story with You.

What prevents you from regularly sharing yourself—feelings, expectations, struggles—with the God who made you and loves you unconditionally? Does the busyness and business of everyday life get in the way? How might your life change if you intentionally shared with God as you would a close friend? Give it a try.

LOVE

God,
I want to experience your love
not know of it
not rely on it
not live in light of it.

I want to feel your love
not as a baby at mother's breast
but
as the beloved with her lover
held, touched, taken
possessed.

I stand before you
yielded, trembling
apprehensive
waiting, wanting—
yours.

Which lines are you most drawn to, most resistant toward in this poem? Are you open to the level of intimacy with God described above? What level of intimacy do you believe God desires? Share any resistance you may have with God and pray to be more fully open to receiving God's all-encompassing love.

Do You Believe?

(Mark 9:23-24)

We had all heard the stories,
healings too numerous to fathom,
thousands fed,
the testimony of lepers,
the blind, the deaf making their rounds
before the Pharisees shut them down,
locked them up.

The healed named Jesus, the healer.
Desperate, I could not believe, yet
I desperately wanted to believe—
I sought him out.

Do you believe? He asked me—
I was caught off guard,
did I believe?

Then, in an instance of unexpected honesty,
I heard myself say, I believe,
help me in my unbelief.
Jesus' eyes said it all—
Faith indeed.
Faith enough.

What does this poem convey about the type of faith Jesus desires? Where do you desire to trust God, but struggle with fully believing? Surrender to God your struggle and your fledgling faith, knowing it might be enough for God.

EARS TO HEAR

(Matthew 11:15, 13:15-16)

The barrage never ending,
no quiet, not a moment of silence,
incessant squawking and squabbling.

Daily we listen to the perpetual bombardment by
    bombastic babblers, prattling politicians,
    frenzied fearmongers,
    damning Democrats, raging Republicans,
    bellowing bureaucrats,
    self-righteous screamers, pontificating pastors,
    each with their deadly rhetoric,
all seeking to fuel a particular fear,
to stoke the flames of hysteria.

Perhaps we have grown weary of hearing,
worn down by this deluge of din,
choosing to plug our ears
while loudly droning *blah, blah, blah*—
Could it be we plug our ears to Jesus too?

Might we also choose to drown out the Spirit's voice,
knowing we will likely be challenged
to step out of the clamor,
listen to the quiet invitation to follow,
gain a life found by losing,
life as a peacemaker, an enemy-lover,
a denial of self that leads to a new self,
picking up one's daily cross,
a life of persecution, righteousness,
seeking first the kingdom of God.

Are your ears plugged by the cacophony
of worldly voices calling you to the good life,

focusing on your circumstances, stirring up strife?
To whom do you listen?
Jesus desires that we have hearing ears,
ears to hear him call us by name,
ears to hear the voice of the Spirit,
to hear God calling us beloved.
To whom do you listen?
Whoever has your ear has your heart.

Who has your ear? How are the messages that grab your attention helping you cultivate the fruits of the Spirit, encouraging you to listen for Jesus? How do you discern if what you are hearing is from the world or the communications of God? What might God be inviting you to add or subtract from your life, in order to cultivate a more attentive sensitivity to the Spirit's leading?

TREASURE

(MATTHEW 6:19-21, LUKE 12:15-21)

Locate me on a plateau
thick fog shrouds the ground
a single tree stripped of all leaves
barren land beneath grey sky
in a cloud of murky gloom.

Drawn to a ravine
I carefully inch forward to the edge.
Through the depressing mist
I dimly see below
acres of endless treasure,
mountains of bewitching riches,
jewels, possessions, yachts,
mansions, money,
the wealth I so desire.

My hunger growing,
I covet this abundance
for myself.

The fog slowly tumbles down the hill
covering this sea of treasure—
I feel sick as all this now seems lost to me.

Soon the fog dissipates
clearing my view of the valley below.
The riches have disappeared,
replaced by miles of trash—
stuff twisted and tarnished,
rusted, stained, bent and broken.

then a trick of the light—

the riches, treasures, instantly appear
as far as the eye can see—another
flicker of light and the scene switches
again miles, mountains of garbage
stuff twisted and tarnished
rusted, stained, bent and broken.

I awaken, my heart revealed.
My masters, my gods, unmasked,
exposed, for what they are—
rubbish!

What things draw your heart away from God, treasures to which you are attached, that you deem necessary for happiness? What is the draw, the promise they represent, the power they exert over you? Explore these attachments with God, seeking freedom from the claim they have on your life. How can you reconnect to the treasures God has for you, become re-grounded in what's important/eternal?

Two Mothers

(Luke 7:11-16)

The widowed mother
cannot believe her eyes.
Smiling, stroking the face of her son,
her worst day became the best.
Without husband, but with hope.
Her son, once dead, is now alive.
Stroking his face, she softly whispers,
Thank you, Jesus.

The day began quite differently.
Friends gathered
to prepare the son for burial,
his body cold to the touch,
lifeless, an empty shell.
Now ready for the processional,
shell of a son lying on the wagon,
ashes to ashes, dust to dust.

Not so fast!

Enter Jesus.
Coming upon this mournful march,
and moved by compassion,
his touch of life reunited
mother and son.
God be praised!
God has come to help his people!

The news spread.
Another woman sitting alone
lost in her grief,
stroking the robe of her dead son,
hears the shocking news.

Trembling with unanswerable questions,
and self-accusations.
Such is the both/and reality of miracles.

Two mothers, one miracle.
One grateful for a son returned to life,
the other drowning in grief and anguish,
struggling to believe
God has come to help his people.

Not all tragic circumstances end miraculously, but God promises to be present with those who weep. How have you experienced God's love, power and presence in your grief? Are you able to be authentic and real with God and your pain, and trust, even when God doesn't change the outcome? How do you think the grieving mother whose son was not raised by Jesus felt? What could you say to the mother whose son was not raised by Jesus? What would you want to say to Jesus?

ROCK THROWERS

(JOHN 8:3-11)

They gather as one,
seeking not to hinder sin,
but catch the sinner in her shame.
They wait, each holds a special stone
chosen for the act, sharp corners,
but a rock too small to kill alone—
murder by committee.

Fueled by self-righteousness,
seeing through log-blinded eyes,
their time has come.
They enter the home
and drag the startled woman from her bed,
leaving the man behind, untouched.
Frightened, naked, she grabs a sheet,
her only thread of dignity.

Bringing her to Jesus,
ready, impatient, they finger their stones.
Jesus, not heeding their frenzy,
stoops down, writing in the dirt.
One word after another—
a rock drops to the ground
and an accuser backs away.
One rock after another,
each self-righteous slayer
sees Jesus writing and slinks away
till none remain.

Jesus looks her in the eyes.
"Has no one condemned you?"
"No one, sir," she replied.
"Neither do I." Now go and live true
to who you are—a daughter of God.

Do certain sins seem more egregious to you than others? To which sins do you tend to turn a blind eye? In the gospel account, Jesus says, "Go and sin no more," but the reflection above changes the message: "Go and live true to who you are—a daughter of God." How are the two messages different, and how are they the same? Can you freely accept God's grace—for this woman, for yourself? What might Jesus be saying to you about your sin and God's grace?

BLEEDING HEARTS

(LUKE 6:32-36, MATTHEW 5:43-48)

Words to degrade, to decry
wrong-headed thinking,
feelings run amok—
yet is not a heart to break?

Is bleeding not the way of Jesus—
bleeding heart, side, feet and hands?
Does Paul not denounce a calloused heart?
Does God not condemn a hardened heart?

Bleeding hearts softened by the love of God
hearts wounded by injustice,
cruelty, enslavement, the marginalization,
the pain of humanity.

Is not our heart to bleed, our love to flow,
like the milk from the breasts of a mother of a newborn—
freely, lavishly—when we hear the cries of humanity?
Bleeding hearts, flowing love—
Jesus love.

Considering the realities of living in a broken world, what breaks your heart? Are you stirred to action? In addition to prayer, how might God be inviting you to demonstrate love in deed and truth? Take a few moments to pray for someone on the front lines of fighting injustice.

ENJOY A CUP WITH JESUS

Enjoy a cup of coffee or tea with Jesus, just as you would with a good friend. Sit down in your own home, sipping and savoring the cup and the conversation. Pay attention to your senses and feelings during this intimate visit and perhaps journal your response.

WHO SINNED?

(JOHN 9:1-3)

Quick to judge, to name
as catastrophic consequence of sin
earthquakes, floods, fires,
even AIDS...
life lived in a binary,
black and white world.

Desperate to make sense
of what has happened—
making pronouncements,
attaching blame, driving people away
from the power, grace and love
of God.

Forgetting God loves the just and unjust.
Sin unable to handcuff God's ability to bring
good out of any situation,
powerless to stop the cascading dominos
of God's love and grace.

Neglecting to remember
that a mountain of crap
when spread out is called fertilizer—
decaying, rotting garbage becomes mulch.
Things are not always as they first seem.

God the master gardener
using the fertilizer of affliction
to produce fruit, to offer hope,
not judgment, to those overwhelmed
by the piles of garbage,
mountains of crap
in their lives, in the world.

Do you try to make sense of the world by attaching spiritual consequences to catastrophic events? What might be the fallout from forgetting God is with us and lovingly involved in the world God created? What sort of circumstances, world events, tend to create a level of God-amnesia, causing you to forget that God is with you, is for you—God is love? Try to remind yourself in difficult times of the truth of God's love and the transforming power reflected above.

I Know What I Know

Who is Jesus?
What would Jesus do?
Responding quickly, grounding
our pronouncements in scriptures,
certain of our translation,
our understanding,
convinced of our veracity,
ours, the final word.
Truth with a capital T!
A truth that often excludes,
vilifies another
while justifying ourselves,
ignoring our shortcomings,
the sins that so easily entangle,
unaware of the self-protecting, value-affirming,
culturally conditioned agenda of our assertions,
oblivious to the gravitational pull
of ubiquitous influences—
upbringing, culture, race, opportunities,
sexuality, gender, economics—
unwilling, unable to hear a different,
or, God forbid, contrary interpretation
that challenges our perspective,
questions our status quo,
contradicts our doctrine.
Like the Pharisees of Jesus' day,
mired in what we believe,
unassailable truths,
irreversible dogma, resistance
to the Way, the Truth
and the Life.

Would you say you are pretty certain regarding your beliefs about Jesus, or are you open to discovery, new understanding? As you are made aware of other possible perspectives, are you open, fearful, defensive, reactive…? What is the possible danger of becoming fixated on your understanding of scripture, of God? Ask God to open your heart to new possibilities and insights.

Silence and Solitude: the Battlefield

you enter stripped down,
naked, not a fig leaf in sight
no titles, no power symbols
no audience to impress

but not empty-handed

you enter with everything you need
to harm, wound, abuse yourself
have a dialogue with doubt
hear the familiar internal voice of shame
the common refrain of condemnation
wounding, scarring words
like a hurricane destroying all in its path
that old inner voice suppressing
the best version of yourself
your greatest enemy, the one within

escaping the trap of pseudo-identity
being who you need to be
opening to the truth of individuality
to be the one you are truly meant to be
discarding demands from within and without
to behave a particular way
or believe specific ideology
buy, own, wear all that shouts
power, wealth, popularity
entering into silence and solitude

at first flailing, drowning in a tsunami of feelings
then, invited to float, lying on your back, facing the Son
the false identities washed away and replaced
body and soul replenished

as you claim your real name
Beloved of God.

What are your feelings concerning silence and solitude? What has been your experience with each? When you consider being naked before God, what comes to mind? Do you have any negative internal messages that God might be able to change in a time of silence and solitude spent owning your identity as the beloved of God? Is that something you feel drawn to? If yes, think of how you might begin to create pockets of time to be alone with God.

RECONCILIATION: STEP ONE

(MATTHEW 18:15, 7:5)

I come privately, hoping to be heard, desiring restoration.
I come in gentleness, owning my shortcomings—the log in my eye.

I come as a peacemaker, desiring what is broken will be mended.
I come because I value this person, our relationship, our community.

I come believing the best, open to a different interpretation.
I come with exposed heart, circumspect, with ears to hear.

I come prayerfully asking God for grace, wisdom and understanding.
I come fully aware of the forgiveness I have received, I am receiving.

I come in gentleness, praying my words reflect a peaceful spirit.
I come unwilling to let sin or misunderstanding have the last word.

I come knowing this may not go well, that I may be mistreated, slandered.
I come with eyes fixed on Jesus, willing to be wounded that love may win.

I come privately, desiring mutual understanding, restoration.
I come in humility, owning my shortcomings—the log in my eye.

How do you feel about conflict, disagreement and wrongdoing? What fears surface when you sense God leading you toward reconciliation? Which of the characteristics above come easily, and which would be more difficult to pull off? As you read this poem did someone come to mind? If so, take this moment to pray for guidance regarding next steps.

SO MUCH NEED

(MATTHEW 14:13-21, JOHN 6:1-13)

The needs are great, overwhelming—
well beyond your meager and dwindling resources

What can you do, what can you offer to a
world drowning in need?

Gasping for hope
flailing to merely survive

Do you turn away
focus on your life, your family

Choosing blindness, deafness
personal comfort and security—

Who could blame you?

Yet compassion bubbles within
empathy banging on the door of your heart

So you turn to Him, offering
what little you have

All fits neatly into
His scarred and sacred hands

Jesus blesses and breaks
your gifts, your heart

You receive back more than you can carry
baskets and baskets more

The needs remain, overwhelming—
still well beyond your meager and dwindling resources

.

Making your way through the crowd you share
what you have to offer

Trusting in the God of the fish and loaves
to bless, break and multiply your offering—you.

Which of your gifts and resources might Jesus be asking you to bring to Him, that Jesus might bless, break and multiply them? Who is Jesus inviting you to serve, minister to, feed?

ADULT FAITH

(JOHN 16:33, 17:15-16)

Maturity
Reason
Ability
Experience
Independence
Pragmatism
Common sense
Street smarts
Worldly Wisdom

Gives way to

Faithfulness
Inspiration
God-wisdom
Learning through loss—
Dependence
Yielded-ness
Trust

Makes way for

In the world but not of the world
Eyes wide open to
Persecution, pain
Brokenness, suffering
Neediness (our own/the world's)
Compassion
Grace.

This reflection differentiates between worldly wisdom and the wisdom of God. What do you think of the premise that these definitions are mutually exclusive? Do you remember a time when the wisdom or insight you sensed coming from God was not in line with the wisdom of the world? How did you know, and what did God teach you? Where in your life do you struggle to be in the world, but not of the world?

THE MAN WITH THE SIGN

(LUKE 18:10-14)

I am left wondering
about the man on the corner
displaying the tattered sign
disclosing a tattered life.
Is his faith in people greater than my own?
Has cynicism not crept into his heart?
Can he still be a glass-half-full guy,
believing in the goodness and generosity
of others, even me—
as I avert my eyes and drive right by,
does he silently pray for me
while watching my taillights disappear?

Sometimes we allow people to be categorized by life circumstances, sexuality, practices or culture, focusing on the differences and forgetting we are all created in God's image and loved by God. How do your reactions and interactions with the marginalized communicate your values? How might your reactions and interactions with others change if you chose to name the truth that this person before you was created by God?

The Stained-Glass Window

(John 10:1-15)

The enormous window
commands attention:
stained-glass Jesus,
bigger than life, just off center.
I reverently gaze on my Good Shepherd,
the sunlight spraying this holy space
with prism rainbows.

I marvel at how fragmented glass
morphs into this tender depiction;
Jesus, a Jewish Shepherd
with white Anglo face?
Still Jesus.
Spending day and night with sheep
alone in the elements,
not weathered?
Somehow "Europeanized,"
yet still the Shepherd, Jesus.

I change my focus
to the sheep sprinkled throughout,
one lovingly draped over His shoulders,
three near His feet like devoted pets,
others a few feet away,
some heads-down, eating,
several further away,
following from afar.
Others seem to have wandered off
perhaps part of the flock
but not engaged—
maintaining a loose connection
to flock and Shepherd.

As I sit bathed in a myriad of colors,
I wonder,
which sheep am I?
which sheep do I want to be?
which sheep do I need to be?
I sit silently, intently listening
for the voice of my Good Shepherd
to call me by name.

Imagine yourself in the light of the stained-glass window described above, and ask yourself: where am I in proximity to Jesus, my Shepherd? Where do I desire to be? Are you able to completely trust God as provider and protector? Are you listening for Jesus to call your name, to lead you? Ask God to help you to have a receptive heart and listening ears?

Words, Words, Words

(Matthew 12:33-37, 5:21-22)

Careless, abusive, empty words
flying freely—
sowing strife,
fostering fear,
fueling attack,
damaging souls.

Exposed motives, values, beliefs
erupting from a heart
filled with anger,
ignited by fear,
unleashing deadly thrusts,
spewing devastation,
laying waste.

Reckoning awaits.
Words testify, with
undisguised honesty,
to a vile heart
filled with evil.

We can use words to powerfully transmit hope and encouragement, but also to cause division and destruction. Are your words most often meant to heal or hurt? When you feel misunderstood or attacked, do your words reflect your fleeting feelings or your unchangeable identity in Christ? What might God be inviting you to recall to heart and mind when you speak, when words hurt you? Ask God to help you to speak words that bring life, insight—words fueled by love of God and others.

THE GREAT ESCAPE

(LUKE 5:16)

months in the planning
the moment has come
nothing left to chance
all at the ready

the internal voice
be productive
this is selfish
what will others think

all conspiring to derail
the painstaking planning
the inner felt need/desire

weeks have turned into days
days into hours
time now being calculated
in minutes and seconds

the vehicle gassed
the hideout secured
escape route set

slow down, be still
opening to God
in spacious unhurriedness
free from frantic harried-ness
from striving, producing, succeeding

free to enter into love
like Jesus, slip away
to soak, savor, linger
release, receive
to be with, to become
to linger with God.

Jesus orchestrated His life around getaways, alone time with God. Creatively consider how you might escape for a few moments, hours, even a day. Take a few minutes to consider what a great escape might look like for you. Start small, entering into whatever space you manage with the intention to be present to the Presence that surrounds you and indwells you. Be open to God's communication in expected and unexpected ways.

A Day with Jesus

You may want to consider planning a date with Jesus. Go for a meal, take a walk together, watch a movie, go for a drive, seeking to be present to and with Jesus. Enjoy His presence and the conversation between you as you would with an intimate friend. Pay attention to the questions that come up—what does Jesus desire you to know about yourself, Him and your relationship with Him?

THE PRODIGALS

(LUKE 15:11-32)

Seemingly out of nowhere
yet building over time
frustration, anger, longing
eruption, confrontation
fracturing the father's heart with
harsh, stinging words
demanding, demeaning, destructive
words.
I wish you were dead,
give me what is mine
so I can go.
Gone then.

Powerful, prosperous,
accustomed to holding on,
even leaving the ninety-nine
to save the one
but not this time.
Sad eyes watch the son
disappear from sight,
lost to him.
Let him go.

Free from family constraints
flush with money
friends flocking to his side
until they didn't.
Funds and friends replaced by pigs,
desperate, hopeless, hungry
alone
but seeing with new eyes.
My father's servants fare better.
I'll plead for mercy.

I must go.
Home then.

Each morning, afternoon, evening
he stands at the door
scanning the horizon
sad eyes, broken heart
pitied by his servants
grieving his son
alone
his precious child lost to him,
gone
as good as dead.

The son rehearses his apology
as he walks
anxious, fearful
uncertain of his reception
ashamed, unworthy
he shuffles home.

The father, scanning the horizon
sees a distant figure.
Could it be?
Jumping to his feet
breathlessly running to see.
My boy!
The son drops to his knees
confessing
the father reaches for him
exulting.
Hugging him close
through tears of joy
he calls the servants—
bring clean clothes,
the family ring for his finger,
sandals on his feet—

we celebrate, feast!
My son dead, now alive,
lost, found.

All rejoice at the return of the son,
dead, now alive
lost, found.
All but one.
The brother who stayed
duty-bound son
filled with
frustration, anger, longing
confrontation soon to erupt
fracturing the father's heart
a son already lost.

Consider being the prodigal returning, and being met with such surprising grace and love of the father; how does it feel to be this celebrated and embraced, especially when you're aware of your sin? What does this reflection communicate about the person of God? With whom do you identify in this poem? Have you been sought by God, or has God allowed you to wander and return? What did you learn about yourself and God's heart during your journey?

FOOTPRINTS IN THE SAND

In my dream I see
two sets of footprints in the sand:
strides long, paths irregular,
prints not perfectly formed.
Playfully running after each other
two lovers chasing intimacy,
laughing, carefree;
the pursuer fueled by desire,
the pursued filled with anticipation.
This a wooing,
a longing to be deeply known,
passionately loved.

Leaping more than running
the pursued beloved stops.
Turning toward the lover,
opening to, receiving from, yielding to,
two drop as one into the sand,
lost in love, tenderly caressing,
offering the gift of self,
each purposefully and delicately opening,
exploring this offered gift.

The waves spraying, splashing,
flowing over the intertwined bodies,
each caress a declaration of love,
value, acceptance and celebration.
Each lost, found and known in love.
God's kingdom come,
God's will now done.

Are you comfortable thinking of God's love in this intimate manner? Is there a boundary you set with God in terms of intimacy? What resistance, if any, arises regarding the interpretation of God as lover, pursuer? If you desire the intimacy with God depicted here, share that desire with God.

GOD'S TIMING

(JOHN 11:1-44)

This is God's plan, God's timing, God's doing—
a trip delayed that brings death.

A timing that seems a tad off,
ill-timed rather that perfect timing.

Oh yes, it all ends gloriously,
life snatched out of the jaws of death.

Yet two sisters grieve, a community mourns,
as death, the last enemy, takes another life.

Mary's words, "if only you had been here, my brother
would not have died," pierce His soul.

Oh yes, all was orchestrated by God,
for God's honor, God's glory, but still...

Finally, Jesus arrives, not jumping ahead
to the finale but entering into the now.

Oh yes, God is in control, God has a plan
but the pain is palpable.

Jesus weeps for His friends, with His friends,
a man of compassion—one who suffers with.

Oh yes, the stone will soon be moved away, Lazarus raised,
God glorified, but for now death hangs heavy in grieving hearts,

and Jesus, the Resurrection and the Life, weeps,
His deep love expressed by cascading tears.

Oh yes, Jesus knows what is to come—
Jesus will soon call forth Lazarus from the tomb,

but for now Jesus weeps, embracing the pain of a broken world,
entering the sorrow and grief of His friends and their community.

Can you think of an experience when God's timing was not what you desired, the outcome not what you hoped for? Have you experienced an occasion when God's timing and initial outcome were not what you desired, but with the passage of time, God used the outcome for good? How do those circumstances inform and shape your ability to trust God?

WHO IS IN?

(MATTHEW 13:24-30)

Selectivity, exclusivity,
snobbery, superiority—
the tendency in all of us
to exclude, compare,
establish gates and gatekeepers,
criteria to determine
who is in and who is out.
We feel called to eliminate undesirables,
hire theological bouncers
to remove the misfits,
those who don't meet the requirements,
measure up.

Jesus counters this contempt by
expanding the concept of neighbor,
employing the use of "our" in His prayer,
embracing the marginalized,
instructing us to cease judging.
Put away your hoe!
Leave the weed-killer in the shed.
Allow the wheat and tares to grow
side by side, watering both.
Let God determine
which are wheat and which are tares,
who is in and who is out.

How do you feel about the idea of letting wheat and tares grow together? What fears surface? Why do you think Jesus instructs us to leave the determination of the identity of wheat and tares to God? As you look at your own life, when do you tend to become judgmental? What issue(s) most often triggers your tendency to exclude? In which areas of your life is God inviting you to be more inclusive, nurturing and accepting?

WHO DO YOU SAY THAT I AM?

(MATTHEW 16:15)

Sweet, sweet Jesus—
tender and terrible
inviting and challenging
calming and confounding
kind not nice
clear yet perplexing.

No down-filled comforter,
a piercing sword
moved by compassion
inflamed by anger
encourager, provoker
2x4-swinging
side-of-the-head-hitting
truth-smacking
status-quo-shattering
hypocrite-bashing
child-welcoming
mother-hen-gathering
grace-giving
Son of God.

Fiercely independent (from religious conventions)
fully dependent on God and Spirit
slipping away for solitude and prayer
giving away self in service and sacrifice.

Healer, weeper, sufferer
water-walker, death-defeater
cross-bearer, foot-washing instigator
leper-healer, sight-restoring
life-giver, faith-renovator—
Bread, Light, Shepherd, Creator

Way, Resurrection, Truth
Alpha, Omega, Beloved of God
crucified, wounded, betrayed
forsaken, victorious.
Sweet, sweet Jesus.

Are you surprised by any of the above descriptions of Jesus? Disturbed or comforted? Who is Jesus to you? Do you have anything to add to the descriptors of Jesus above? Choose a characteristic of Jesus that speaks to you at this moment and carry it with you throughout your day.

Bid Me to Come

(Matthew 14:22-33)

Yes, step out of the boat
join me on the water, Peter.
That's it—one leg at a time
Steady now, stand tall.

Look at me.
We can do this.
NO! Look at me!
Focus on me
my voice,
my presence.

Yes, yes, there are
wind and waves—
always will be in
this broken world.

Look at me—
quieter of storms,
feeder of thousands,
healer, raiser of the dead
the One with you now.

Look here, stay focused—
even, especially, as the wind grows
in intensity, the waves in size.
Fear not, I AM with you.

Peter, the rock, fix your
eyes on me and you
will not sink.

We always have the choice to let our circumstances take our focus toward God or away from God. What are the wind and waves in your life right now? How might keeping your eyes on Jesus steady your heart and mind? Turn your attention toward God in prayer right now. What crazy, courageous thing might Jesus be inviting you to join Him in doing?

PETER, GOD AND SATAN

(MATTHEW 16:13-23)

"Who do you say I am?"
the question.

"You are the Christ,
the Son of the living God."

Such clarity, certainty—
hearing ears
awareness of God's words, wisdom
an open conduit to God
truth beyond human knowing
a mind set on things above.

Such certainty often fleeting
faith dissipating
like the morning fog.

"God forbid it, Lord! This shall never happen to You."

Again such clarity, certainty
unaware of the internal shift
to human knowing
the eternal perspective lost.
God's interests swapped out
for human wants—
a mind set on earthly things,
ears clogged to God's voice
faith dissipating
like the morning fog.

Jesus' response is immediate,
with clarity, certainty
"Get behind me, Satan."

Conviction is not necessarily a litmus test that something is God's wisdom. We might be clearly and certainly in God's will one moment, and just as clearly out of step with God the next. When have you been tempted to swap out God's interests for your own?

THANK GOD

(LUKE 18:9-14; MATTHEW 7:1-2, 7:5; REVELATION 3:17)

It sneaks in unnoticed—judgment.
A person's appearance, skin color,
vocabulary, political views,
job, criminal record, language, accent,
citizenship, country of origin,
title, status, ZIP code, clothes,
purse, watch, shoes.

It can happen before we know it—
better than, more honorable, righteous.
Thank God we aren't like them.
Parading our degrees, titles,
accessories of status, for all to see
we are respectable, successful, productive,
making our way in the world.

It can happen before we know it—
like the rich young ruler, we believe
we have fulfilled all God requires.
Like the Pharisee, deaf to the Gospel,
blinded by our riches, our comfort and ease,
unable to see for the planks in our eyes
or hear Jesus' message of love.

It can happen before we know it—
Judged as we judge and found wanting,
unable to see our own poverty,
to recognize our great need
for God's unconditional love, mercy, grace.

Do you tend to judge others—individuals or people groups? Even if you aren't vocal about your opinions, do you allow judgment to occupy your thoughts? It can happen easily and quickly. Ask God to make you aware of such a tendency and replace it with a heart of compassion, care and sensitivity.

END OF THE DAY

(MATTHEW 20:1-15)

The morning mist long dissipated,
the sun dangling in the sky
like a thousand-watt light bulb,
rivers of sweat on foreheads, necks,
running down bent backs.

The truck approaching in the distance
creating a storm of dust,
horn beep, beep, beeping,
bed filled to overflowing with latecomers.
A hum of grace begins in me.

Seeing the truck, my heart leaps.
This will be one of my favorite days!
Those late hires have no idea
what the end of the day will bring:
confusion, bewilderment, joy!

Anticipating that moment,
I relive my own experience,
the mind-blowing, life-altering,
gracious generosity extended me,
from my supervisor then,
now mentor, friend.

The late hires jump from the truck,
receive their tools and instructions.
We who have been working since morning,
wearing the sweat and grime of our labor,
exchange knowing glances,
anticipating the end of the day,
the hum of grace growing in intensity.

The hours pass quickly.

Soon the finishing bell sounds,
the ring a chorus of angels.
The end of the workday signals
a time to be paid, a good day's pay
for a good day's work.

Knowing what will transpire,
I rush to the front where I can see the faces.
Last arrivals called first,
come, receive your pay.
I watch as she hands out the envelopes,
watch them counting and recounting the money
looking around, uncertain.
Is it a mistake or a miracle?

They quietly talk among themselves,
discovering each has received
a full day's pay.
The realization slowly dawning,
each smudged face now awash with joy,
gift of grace perceived,
gratefully received.

Once again I share around the dinner table
stories of the goodness I have seen.
My boss, my friend, my lord
continues to amaze with lavish generosity.
I pray tomorrow brings
another late afternoon truck
beep, beep, beeping,
heralding, anticipating, day-end grace.

How have you seen and experienced God's grace in your own life and in the lives of those you love? What particular grace of God are you experiencing right now? How has your experience of God's grace shaped your life, your view of your circumstances, your interactions with others? Take a moment to ask God to help you hear the hum of grace around you today.

Jesus Eyes, Jesus Ears

(John 5:19, 5:30)

The world is a noisy, bustling
blaring, thunderous
ear splitting, deafening place.

The world is a busy
frantic, frenetic, frenzied
eye-distorting, blinding place.

Distractions, racket, clatter and clamor
like the crashing waves of the ocean
never ending, pounding and pounding.

In the midst of this craziness
Jesus saw what his Father was doing
Jesus heard what the Father was saying

I want Jesus eyes, Jesus ears—
eyes seeing the eternal in the midst of the temporal,
ears that hear the voice of God amid the din.

Eyes that see the fingerprints of God
in dire circumstances, among the marginalized,
in places of injustice and brokenness,
in a twinkling star, among the lilies of the field.

Ears that hear the voice of Jesus
calling me by name, inviting me to follow,
recognizing Jesus' voice
among the voices of others, in the voice of others,
in the crackling of a burning bush,
in the wind.

Remove the calluses on my heart
the cataracts in my eyes
that I may have Jesus eyes, Jesus ears.

Do you believe God communicates with you individually? Why or why not? When have you sensed communication from God? What circumstances or practices contributed to your awareness of God's voice? What currently may be hindering your ability to see what God is doing or to be tuned in to what God is communicating? What do you need to change to learn to discern the communications of God?

Two Words

(John 11:35)

"Jesus wept"

Jesus grieves with me
Jesus embraces my sorrow, me
Jesus doesn't rush to resurrection truth
Jesus sits with me in my now
    feels with me
    hurts with me.

Jesus weeps.

    An invitation to tarry in my grief
    An invitation to embrace my
        anguish
            questions
                anger
                    confusion
    my felt reality, honestly and openly.

Jesus cares.
Jesus is with me,
        knowing my pain
          knowing me
             freeing me to feel
                reminding me that I am not alone.

Hallelujah!

What do the tears of Jesus reveal about the person of God? Is it comforting for you to know Jesus feels what we feel, grieves along with us? When in your life do you think Jesus has suffered sadness/despair with you/for you? Secure in that knowledge, you can bring all your emotions and your deepest pain honestly and openly before God. Spend some time sharing your heart with Jesus.

GOD OR OTHERS

(JOHN 5:41, 5:44, 12:43)

The innate desire to be liked,
to be seen as successful,
to feel valued, heard, affirmed.

It is easy to lose oneself,
to subjugate one's voice,
one's truths, even God's truth,
in order to be liked, accepted.

This battle if not fought is
already lost—a simple question
opens the heart to this—who
is your audience: God or others?

Choosing to accept the praise of others
is to bolster the power of their criticism—
Jesus did not accept praise from men.
Jesus lived to do God's will,
to speak God's truth,
to follow the Spirit's leading
regardless of
the reactions of others.

The Pharisees loved praise from others,
more than praise from God,
thus were blinded to
the presence of God in their midst.

For whom do you perform?
To whom do you look for praise,
validation, sense of worth?
God or others?

Who is your audience, God or others?

To whom do you look for praise and validation? In which arenas do you tend to be more concerned about the opinions of others? Where do you feel most free to be yourself, the person God has called and created you to be? Prayerfully consider the statement that to desire praise is to empower criticism.

Writing Poetry

You have been reading these daily offerings for a while now, and if you are anything like me, the following thought, no matter how fleeting, has most likely crossed your mind: I can do this. You might have dismissed it immediately, or needed to get on with your day, but today I'm inviting you to give it a try. Choose a familiar gospel passage you enjoy and rewrite it as a free verse poem.

You can do this. You don't need to complete it today—take your time and have some fun. Leave it for a while and come back to it another day. Take poetic license with the story and the verse; freely create, as God, the creator and loving parent, delights in your efforts.

THE LEAST OF THESE

(MATTHEW 25:35-40)

Created by God—
valued, significant,
loved by God.

Dirty fingers,
shabby clothes,
sun-darkened skin,
reeking BO,
standing on the corner—
resting on a bench,
a makeshift sign,
vacant eyes,
desperate.

Do you see them
truly see them
or do you ignore them—
assuming you know their story.

How this is all their fault—
how it will not, could not, happen to you,
how they will misuse whatever gift,
if any, you choose to give them?

Do you acknowledge
they have parents, a name, a story—
are a person created by God,
valued, significant, loved by God?

Do you see Jesus standing with them,
desperate, hands outstretched,
shabby clothes,
sun-darkened skin,
reeking BO,

pleading eyes,
inviting you to love?

What might change in your posture and attitude toward the homeless, if you began to see Jesus standing with them? Ask God to help you to see with new eyes, to see others as creations of God, those whom Jesus came to love and set free.

LEAVING YOU

(JOHN 14:16, 14:26, 16:7-11, 16:17-20)

Leaving?
You are leaving us for good?
Not like the times you've slipped away,
unwilling to be found?
You are actually leaving,
going to a place we are not able to go?

We have left everything—
families, careers,
friends, possessions—
to follow you, to be with you.
We believed in you,
learned from you, ate with you,
walked with you.
All for what?
You have the audacity to say
it will be better?
Better for whom?

It is for our good that you leave us.
You have made some perplexing,
unsettling statements before,
but this, this is a slap in the face,
a punch to the gut.

You are our teacher.
We chose to follow you.
Now you tell us
you will send another, but...
your invitation, your CALL was,
"Follow ME,"
not some stand-in,

substitute,
understudy.

Yes, yes, this one who is to come
sounds grand—an advocate
to remind us of your teaching,
to expose error, to teach us more,
but he/she will not be,
cannot be you.

How can you leave us?
Don't you care about us?
Are we no longer important to you?
Are we too much for you,
such a drain that you are
no longer willing to put up with us?
Have we not measured up?
Have we failed you, disappointed you?
Is it all Peter's fault, my fault?

I believe, help me in my unbelief—
a prayer caught in my throat,
jammed down by sorrow.
Crushed by feelings of abandonment,
I am bereft, confused, distraught,
forlorn.

Imagine the feelings of the disciples as they hear that after three years of faithfully following Jesus, Jesus is abandoning them. Jesus promised them the Holy Spirit, but they couldn't imagine a spirit replacing the person they had seen perform miracles day after day. Jesus said it would be easier for them, but they had no relationship with the Holy Spirit. What is your relationship with the Holy Spirit? Do you think it would be easier for you to follow Jesus if Jesus were physically walking with you? What would it look like to walk through your day with an intentional openness to and awareness of the Holy Spirit in your life?

LETTING GO

(MATTHEW 10:26-31, 14:27)

We hold on to the edge
fearful of letting go, of falling,
failing, letting others down—
landing on the cold, hard, ungiving ice.

Frightened, anxious, uncertain,
we hold on all the tighter to what we know,
have been taught, is generally accepted—
never experiencing the gliding freedom
a thin blade on ice makes possible.

Our communities—cold, rigid,
fearful, frightened,
unable to experience the gliding freedom
that Jesus offers us.

Yet Jesus calls to us
even as He called to Mary at the tomb,
His disciples, the Pharisees, all those
with ears to hear, eyes to see.

Let go of your certitude, rigidity,
presumptions, traditions, institutions,
rituals, customary practices, the tried and true,
religion as you know it.

But fear of falling, failing,
being rejected, ostracized, persecuted paralyzes—
we do not let go,
we are not experiencing the gliding freedom
that Jesus offers us.

Can you hear Jesus' invitation?
Wil you choose to drink the new wine,

embrace His life-freeing, life-giving truths,
"You have heard it said,
but I say to you" truths that Jesus speaks today?

Jesus waits a few feet from the railing
hand outstretched, just out of reach—
inviting you to let go.

What feelings arise as you considering letting go of something that has served you well in the past? What may God be inviting you to let go of because it is no longer helpful in your relationship with God? What new wine and new wineskins is Jesus inviting you to embrace?

TRANSFIGURATION

(MATTHEW 17:1-13)

Something wild just happened,
totally unexpected,
incomprehensible, unexplainable,
the God of surprises surprises
during a time of prayer,
a time of turning aside,
opening their hearts, lives to God.

The curtain pulled back
Jesus brilliantly transfigured—
his face blinding as the sun,
his clothing a dazzling white,
human or divine, sacred or secular
divided no longer.
Transcendence and immanence
same time and place,
taking up the same space.

Moses and Elijah stop by
the Old and New linked—
a time beyond words
beyond time and space,
yet in time and space.

Peter shatters the moment,
let's do something, make something,
commemorate this event!
The perceived need to do for God
rather than be with God.

Clouds form, shadows heighten,
Papa proudly proclaims,

This is my beloved son
with whom I am well-pleased.
Listen to him.

The God of surprises surprises those with Jesus. The divinity of Jesus revealed. The fullness of God, fullness of man revealed—not in opposition to one another, but in harmony, unified. Are you more comfortable with the manifestation of Jesus as man or as the Christ? What are the positive aspects of the immanence of Jesus (one with us and one like us) and the transcendence of Jesus, the Christ (His otherness)? Which one do you prefer, or more often pray to? How might Jesus be inviting you to integrate both?

I AM (ego eimi)*

Since the beginning
I was with God.
In me is life,
Life that is light
illuminating the darkness within,
a light unable to be overcome.

I became flesh,
making known
the true nature of God,
the fullness of God dwelling in me,
a living imprint of God's being,
invisible God made visible.

I AM the Bread of Life
offering life in abundance,
offering my very flesh for you.

I AM the Light of the World
shining forth God's love,
offering hope, extending God's grace.

I AM the Gate
providing entry into new relationship
with God and neighbor.

I AM the Good Shepherd
offering to lead you, calling you by name.
giving my life for you.

I AM the Resurrection and the Life
announcing hope and life
even in death.

I AM the Way, the Truth and the Life—
all that you need, desire,
is found in me.

I AM the Vine
connecting you to me, to God,
your source of sustenance, life.

I AM the Alpha and the Omega,
the beginning and the end,
who is, who was and who is to come.

---

*I want to point out a significance concerning these seven "I am" statements, which is not easily discerned in the English translation. The Greek words *ego eimi* are used to introduce each of the above proclamations. I am not a Greek scholar, but I do know just enough Greek to be useful. The usage of *ego eimi* communicates that what follows is a declarative statement of the essence of the one spoken of. Thus each of these statements is not simply a general description of who Jesus is—tall, short, skinny, heavy—but rather a profound revealing of who Jesus most truly is. In addition, this Greek construction *ego eimi* mirrors the same usage found in the Greek translation of the Old Testament (LXX—the Septuagint), specifically Exodus 3, where God declares God's name to Moses. **Thus, the New Testament "I am" statements imply the deeper, more profound truth that Jesus is God.**

To which of the *I am* statements are you most drawn? What does this truth reveal to you about Jesus and about God's involvement in your life that you need to know and experience today? What feelings do these pictures of the person of God and God's involvement stir within you? As you reflect on the totality of the *I am* of Jesus, how can this help you to keep your eyes on Jesus throughout your day, life?

LOVE POURED OUT

(MATTHEW 26:6-13, MARK 14:3-9, LUKE 7:36-50, JOHN 12:1-8)

Bravely, she enters
a man's house, a man's world
where she has no place,
disregarded and excluded.

Fearlessly, she approaches
carrying a treasure,
an alabaster jar
of precious perfume.

Lovingly, she comes,
emboldened by her love
fueled by her resolve
to honor Jesus.

It is love that emboldens her, love that
fuels her resolve, propels her forward.

She breaks open love's gift,
foreshadowing his broken body—
the precious perfume flowing freely
as will his blood.

She loses herself in love,
conveying without words,
her feelings, her devotion,
not caring what others think, say;
"a waste, a meaningless, sentimental gesture."

Jesus sees it differently—
"Truly I say to you,
wherever this gospel is preached in the whole world,

what this woman has done
will also be spoken of in memory of her."

Jesus receives love's anointing.

What do you admire about this woman? How do you describe her outpouring of feelings for Jesus? How did her feelings empower her to live and love? When have you been emboldened by love to do something risky or vulnerable that others may not have understood? What are your feelings toward Jesus? How do your feelings empower you to live and love? How might you demonstrate your love for Jesus today?

BE LOVED

be one who is loved
deeply
perfectly
tenderly
powerfully
simply
profoundly

Do you see yourself as one passionately, infinitely loved by God? How would you live differently if you lived as the beloved of God? Seek to be mindful of this truth, that you are beloved of God, recalling it throughout your day and paying attention to how it has an impact on your interactions with others.

Blessed Is He

(Luke 19:29-40)

a beast of burden,
proudly on parade,
carries the sole dignitary
in this royal procession

palm leaves waving,
people shouting,
rocks quivering,
hoping for the chance
to cry out, to declare
what all creation knows
to be true—

Hosanna, Hosanna
Blessed is he who comes
in the name of the Lord.

These same voices will soon be crying out, "Crucify him, crucify him!" Do you experience swings in your enthusiasm to follow Jesus? How do you resist getting caught up in the energy of the crowd and instead remain true to what you believe and trust about Jesus?

THE MADNESS OF JESUS

(WHO ELSE DO YOU SAY I AM?)

No status-quo,
play-it-safe,
two-birds-in-the-bush-
worth-one-in-the-hand,
populous-pleasing,
cross-at-the-corner,
scouts'-honor,
do-gooder—

but a risk-taking
boundary-breaking
jay-walking
rabble-rousing
new-wine-in-new-skins
"you have heard it said,
but I say to you"-teaching
come-with-a-sword
fire-starting
turn-man-against-father,
daughter-against-mother
let-the-dead-bury-the-dead
sell-all-you-have
cut-off-your-hand
pluck-out-your-eye
equal-to-God-claiming
Sabbath-shattering
enemy-loving
leper-touching
woman-elevating
Samaritan-welcoming
Pharisee-condemning
life-giving

death-embracing
Word of God.

Which words, if any, in the above poem surprise you, disturb, comfort you? Which line is your favorite? Why? What is this poem seeking to communicate about the person of Jesus? How does it describe the Jesus you know, the Jesus you need in your life right now? In what areas in your life may Jesus be wanting to challenge/expand your thinking, your beliefs regarding who Jesus is?

Stop, Look and Listen

Having reached the end of this section, take some time to go back and review your journal using one or more of the prompts below. You may want to do this over a few days.

Word/Phrase

Write the words/phrases/questions that stood out to you in the previous reflections, thoughts that drew you in or caused resistance, affected you positively or negatively, moved you in some way. Try using different colored pens to represent different emotions. Pay attention to and make note of your feelings, listening for the invitations or challenges from God.

Exploring Themes

Attempt to discover what message(s) God has for you. What might God be inviting or challenging you to embrace, live into? If a particular theme surfaces, consider the nature of it. Is it more of an invitation (something you long for and welcome) or a challenge (something to overcome)?

What do you notice about Jesus through these poems and questions? Does anything surprise you? How might your feelings toward or your experience of Jesus be shifting, expanding, deepening?

SECTION THREE

JESUS' DEATH AND RESURRECTION

RECEIVING

(John 13:5)

slipping away
Jesus returns with towel and basin
looking more like servant
than leader

Jesus kneels before me—
I freeze as he removes
my sandals
embarrassed, nervous
uncertain what to do

Jesus' pace is slow
his actions purposeful,
gentle,
tenderly washing,
drying my feet

his touch
his pace
invite me to be present,
open

my body relaxes
my awkwardness dissolves
I begin to receive
opening to Jesus' touch,
Jesus' presence, in new ways

rising to his feet
he touches my shoulder
his hand lingering there

Jesus leans in
his mouth near my ear

I feel his breath
as Jesus whispers
his words unlock my heart

tears stream down my face
I am lost in the moment
I am lost in his love—
seen, known

Imagine yourself in this poem, Jesus coming to you, kneeling before you, washing and drying your feet. What do you feel? What do you desire, what do you need Jesus to say to you?

ONE OF YOU WILL BETRAY ME

(MATTHEW 26:20-22)

His words break the mood,
break into the hidden parts
of my heart.

I wonder, no I fear
I may be the one,
I may be the betrayer

fear escalating, I blurt out
"Is it I?"

Yearning for release, absolution
knowing I could be the one,
fearing I will be the one.

What, if any, concern do you have regarding your motivation, desire or commitment to follow Jesus? Honestly share your feelings with Jesus while owning God's love for you and God's presence with you, within you.

Denial

"I will never fall away!
I will never deny you!"

embolden by Peter's hubris
I avoid honest reflection

like Adam and Eve before me
opting for covering, hiding

hurriedly blurting
"I will not deny you"

now no need to explore
my exposed heart.

Are there parts of your heart you want to keep hidden from God? What hinders you from believing God loves you in your struggles, in your worst moments? Soak in God's love and, when you are ready, share those heart places where you are hiding from God with God.

THE GARDEN

(MATTHEW 26:36-46)

"follow me"
his words carry me back
to the dawn of our journey
and again I follow
together we move slowly
as if crossing a muddy field
finally arriving at the garden

"watch and pray"
his eyes pleading
beads of red-tinged sweat
breaking upon his brow

he moves just steps away
drops to the ground
his voice strained
his breathing labored

"If possible...
not my will but your will be done"

suddenly he is standing before me
"could you not keep watch with me
for even an hour?"

Jesus returns to his prayers
and I to my sleep.

As you read this poem, what are your feelings toward the disciples? Toward Jesus? Jesus honestly and openly shares His reluctance with God. Is there anything on your heart that you have not yet voiced to God?

Notice that Jesus called three people to be with Him in this time of struggle, a good reminder of our need for others in our lives. Who are the people who have been with you in times of need? Take a minute to write a note, email or text expressing your gratitude.

The Tomb, the Garden, the Cross

(John 11:35, Luke 22:42-44, Mark 15:34)

Be brave, strong, stoic.
Don't cry,
God has a plan.
What doesn't kill you...

Words meant to temper feelings,
imprison thoughts, bury pain,
prescribing, demanding restraint
of sorrow, honest emotion.

Stand tall, don't question
no uncertainty, wavering, anger,
no outbursts, no tears.
What doesn't kill you...

Yet, Jesus wept,
sweat blood in the garden,
asked God for another way,
cried out in agony from the cross.

Jesus' feelings freely flowing,
raw, unedited honesty before God.
Trust, faith, utter dependence,
demonstrating freedom to feel, question,
cry out to God.

Are you always honest with God? Are you able to be angry, question, express disappointment or frustration (all emotions recorded throughout scripture)? Take a few moments to open your heart to God, living into God's compassionate presence with you and unending love for you. What do you desire to cry out to God?

More Than a Sword

(John 18:1-12)

The realization dawning,
this cannot be happening,
everything going sideways,
coming to an end.

Peter, unable to believe
Jesus' predictions
of death and denials—
His kingdom not of this world?!

Under cover of darkness
the captors come,
Judas in the lead,
betrays Jesus with a kiss.

Peter, reaching for his sword,
seeks to seize the moment,
a weapon to exert his will,
further his desired end.

Peter's sword a symbol
of worldly ways and wisdom,
affirmation of his devotion
to a personal agenda.

Swinging at a temple guard,
sowing seeds of rebellion,
hoping for a revolution,
severing a servant's ear.

"Put away your sword."
Jesus heals the damage done
by Peter's selfish act.
"Shall I not drink the cup my father gives?"

Do you sometimes see a little of yourself in Peter? In which area(s) of your life do you wield the sword of your own agenda? Are you willing to lay down your sword and trust in the timing and wisdom of Jesus? What does it look like to surrender that to God?

JUDAS

(MATTHEW 26:47-49, 27:1-5)

Vilified, demonized,
his actions nothing like mine,
branded as utterly other,
not me,
not who I might be.

Judas, traitor, betrayer,
one to shun, run from, or perhaps
an unwelcome mirror
of who we could become, or are?
Judas, not a cautionary tale,
but a wake-up call to all who follow Jesus.

Judas, did you always know
you would betray God's Son
for silver?
Judas, did you always know
you would betray Him with a kiss?

Jesus, who walked on water,
restored sight, healed lepers,
cripples, sick, the deaf.
Jesus, who calmed the storm,
raised the dead, fed thousands,
freed captives, full of grace,
truth, light and life.

Judas, did you know
your heart would change,
betrayal not your final moment,
but regret?
Drowning in remorse,

thirty silver pieces scorned,
rope and tree, your answer to shame.

Judas, did you cry to Jesus,
as the thief hanging beside Him
would shortly plead?
Did you dare cry out to the One betrayed?

Judas, did you come to know
Jesus' forgiveness? Grace?
As the noose tightened,
did memories of friendship
flood your mind?
As you struggled for breath,
did you cry out to the One betrayed?
And did He answer,
"Today you will be with Me in paradise"?

As you struggled for your final breath,
Judas, did you finally come to know
forgiveness, peace?
When your arms and legs flailed no more,
your lifeless body still,
did you open your eyes
and see the One betrayed
welcome you into paradise?

As you read this meditation, what feelings surfaced? Have you ever considered the possibility that Judas may have been forgiven by Jesus? Spend time reflecting on God's total and absolute forgiveness and acceptance of you, letting it flow into a time of gratitude and thanksgiving.

Moving Toward the Cross

(Luke 22:39-46)

The garden now deserted,
small pools of blood marking Jesus' agony,
reminders of his struggle with the Father's will.
Yes, Jesus said yes,
and the dominos of death began to fall—
the kiss, the trials, the beatings,
the mocking, the nails, the spear.

In the gruesome events of Good Friday
it is difficult to hear the hum of grace,
but his love-song for us reaches a glorious crescendo
with the words,
"Father, into your hands I commit my spirit."
Jesus breathes his final breath.

It was love that compelled Jesus forward,
gave him the strength to go on,
sustained and empowered him.
Jesus' desire for you and me
to be in relationship with the Triune God
to be a part of the eternal dance of Love
known as the Trinity.

Good Friday, a blood-stained valentine
declaring Jesus' love for us,
a love poured into the hearts of all
who have placed their trust in his sacrifice.

Are you able to empathize with Jesus, knowing even Jesus struggled with His Father's will? Do you struggle with trusting God, believing God's will is ultimately good? How do you find God's will in hopelessness or uncertainty or when painful circumstances arise? What does this poem convey about God's love?

Before Caiaphas

(Matthew 26:57-58)

False witnesses on parade,
lies masquerading as truth
Jesus remains silent.

"Are you the Christ,
the Son of God?"
Jesus responds.

Anger erupts—
"BLASPHEMY!
He deserves death."

Spiting in his face,
beating him,
slapping him.
"Prophesy to us,
who is it that
strikes you
spits on you
slaps you?"

Jesus is silent.

How do you feel about Jesus remaining silent in the face of such unfairness? What do you long for Him to say or do? What might God be seeking to teach you through Jesus' example?

SIMON

(MARK 15:21)

a spectator
drawn by the commotion
now a participant

chosen by a Roman guard
to carry a cross

a religious pilgrim
now ritually unclean
unable to participate
in the Passover
he had journeyed to celebrate

a person
in the wrong place
at the wrong time

an unwilling disciple
a prisoner of circumstance
a pawn of the powerful

years later
he would look back on that day
and give thanks

a person
in the right place
at just the right time

I walked with Jesus.

When in your life did circumstances turn out to be different from what they seemed? What does that memory teach you about God, about your ability to fully perceive God's reality in the here and now? Ask God to help you to see the invisible, the eternal, to trust, as you continue to walk with Jesus.

The Denial Strategy

(John 18:12-27)

I will not deny you
I will fight to the death
a severed ear
a testimony to my resolve
the depth of my commitment

the others, cowards

I follow
(at a distance)
plotting a daring rescue

the others, long gone
but I am here
with Jesus
awaiting the right moment
to leap into action

"Are you one of his disciples?"
sensing her ruse to unmask me
to foil my plan
I strategically deny being a disciple

two others ask the same
each of my strategic denials
grows in intensity
my plan will not be thwarted
my identity must remain hidden

the cock crows
my facade fades
my grandiosity gutted
my self-deception and cowardliness
mock me

It's possible to continue to commit to a course of action but lose sight of your original motivation. What feelings surface as you notice Peter's concern for his own well-being? For maintaining his self-deception, his self-image? Where might you have this temptation?

Ask God to show you if you have gotten off track, drifting from a good beginning to what is no longer a God-honoring path. Remember, this is about awareness, not condemnation. If you discover you have become misdirected, ask God to help you make a course correction or even to start a new journey.

GOLGOTHA

(JOHN 19:17)

A place of humiliation
rejection
death

A place of forgiveness
love
trust

"Father forgive them…
today you will be with me in paradise,
behold your mother, your son,
weep not for me…"

suffering unable to impede Divine love

anguish, abandonment
"my God, my God…"
powerless to eradicate trust

"Father into your hands…"
bowing his head
Jesus dies.

What feelings arise as you consider a God who allows the ugliness of rejection, evil, violence and death to bring about the beauty of redemption, a God who loves restoration? What does the poem reveal about the power of God's love? What are the challenges and invitations inherent in the words and actions of Jesus from the cross? What would it look like to walk through today seeking to trust in the power of God's love, no matter the circumstances in which you might find yourself?

JESUS, BELOVED OF GOD

(MATTHEW 26:28)

Spring of healing, wholeness and life,
nailed to a cross by
MY sins,
MY rebellion,

affixed to the cross by
YOUR love for me
pierced, crushed,
beaten, bruised,
forsaken by God
all for love.

Love poured into my heart,
rooting me,
grounding me
in love,
challenging me
to love.

What feelings arise as you reflect on the love of God displayed by Jesus' willingness to relinquish, endure, suffer for your sake? What would you like to say to Him in light of this tangible expression of sacrificial love? How does this same love, poured into you, inform and shape your love for others, your interactions with others?

TAKE A WALK WITH JESUS

Although we understand walking alone is often an opportunity to pray, we may not realize that a walk in itself can become prayer. Here's how:

- Walk slowly and deliberately, using all of your five senses as you go.
- Notice how your body moves, how it supports you, how much energy is expended in order to walk. In this moment, how do you feel? Do you have pain? Do you feel pleasure? Does the exercise feel tedious or tiring?
- Notice the light, the warmth of the sun, the air on your skin, the colors surrounding you.
- Begin to notice greater detail in patterns, shapes, textures around you, the shades and contrasts of color, the juxtapositions and relations created by what you see in your surroundings.
- Touch and feel. Pick up stones, twigs, earth, leaves and hold them gently.
- Try to stop thinking and simply be. Let everything drop away; try to be totally present to your sensations.
- Begin to notice smells more acutely: the scent of growing things, of the earth itself.
- Listen to the range of sounds: far-off distant sounds, immediate or close sounds, even your own breathing.
- You may want to keep a memento from your walk, something you particularly enjoyed or that holds meaning for you.
- You may wish to end your walk by journaling, consciously noting what feelings and thoughts came to you during your prayer walk.
- Perhaps you want to end with a thanksgiving exercise, specifically listing gifts God offered you during your walk.

GOOD FRIDAY

(MATTHEW 27:45, 28:2)

the earth quakes in disapproval
the sun hides her face
ashamed to witness today's proceedings
darkness descends like judgment
the air is cold, the intense cold that
precedes the dawning of a new day

Despair and hope often exist side by side. How does it feel to experience this darkness without a sign of light? What is God showing you about your sin, about forgiveness and the surpassing greatness of God's love?

SUFFERING SERVANT

(MATTHEW 20:17-19)

betrayed
insulted
humiliated
wounded
crucified
forsaken by God

Love embodied,
Grace on display.

How are suffering and love interrelated? Which type of suffering mentioned above is hardest for you to bear? How have you suffered or sacrificed for another? Who are you currently led to love in a way that involves denial of self? Ask God to help you extend Christ-like love to others.

Holy Saturday

(John 20:19a)

huddled together
what ifs, if onlys
gnawing at their hearts

fear, anger, hopelessness
alternating as partners
dancing to death's dirge

they wait for what,
for whom
no one is quite sure

sighs of despair shattering the silence,
sadness visible in vacant eyes

it is finished
all is lost.

This is the agonizing in-between place—the now, not yet—of faith. Put yourself into this huddled group of mourners. How are you feeling in this place of despair? Can you continue to trust God or are you tempted to make something happen on your own? Share your feelings with God.

WOMEN AT THE TOMB

(LUKE 24:1-12)

Dressed in black, they approach the tomb,
a trail of tears, a pilgrimage of grief.
Carrying spices to anoint His corpse,
a final act of devotion, love.

One last chance to caress His hands,
to gaze again on His holy face,
to honor His life with burial spices,
whispers of love, goodbyes,
I will carry You, Your words within me.

The stone has been moved.
Entering, they collapse.
The tomb is empty, Jesus is gone.
"Where have they taken Him?"

Bereft, weeping, they grieve their loss,
longing for one more moment,
one last act of devotion and love.

Remember His promise?
Remember His words?
The angel explains what has occurred.

Excited, breathless, giddy, they run
to tell the disciples, tell the world—
He is not there, He is alive!
Jesus has risen! Jesus lives!

How does your love, devotion and desire to serve Jesus shape your actions? Can you think of a time when your desire to love and serve Jesus led you to an unexpected discovery about or encounter with God?

LET ME GO

(JOHN 20:15-17)

Sometimes what seems like orthodoxy can be
a well-hidden and well-disguised heresy.

Despairing, she hears
the familiar voice of Jesus,
"Mary."
Rabbi!
Her heart testifying to
what the mind cannot fathom.

She rushes to Jesus
seeking to hold on to what was
but is no more.
"Mary,
do not cling to me.
Let go, I must ascend."

Mary,
do not hold on to the old,
expand your mind,
transcend what was—
dualistic life-and-death thinking—
that fosters judgment,
hinders creativity.
Embrace the new.

Free me to be I AM,
that I might free you to live.

Like Mary, are you more comfortable holding on to what you already know and appreciate about Jesus? Consider letting Jesus ascend beyond the finite categories of your thinking—is the prospect of a new Jesus concerning or exciting? How would it feel to allow Jesus to comfort you in this?

ON THE ROAD

(LUKE 24:13-35)

Two men lost in their sorrow,
the latest victims
of religious maneuverings,
political placating,

nails driven through their dreams,
their hope pierced—now dead.
Weary, dejected,
they slog home.

He joins them,
a stranger, seemingly unaware
of all that has transpired.

He speaks
and their hearts burn within.

Dare they believe?
Hope in the improbable,
even the impossible?

They invite him to sup with them.

In the breaking of bread
they see Jesus.

Then he is gone
and, like the shepherds in the fields,

they rush to share
all they have heard and seen,
   their dreams resuscitated
   their hope resurrected
   their sorrow replaced
by joy!

Where in your life do you find it difficult to recognize Jesus? When have you sensed your heart burning, yet still had trouble believing that God was communicating with you? What kept you from believing? Celebrate the times when you have recognized, experienced and responded to Jesus.

WOUNDS

(JOHN 20:24-29)

a glorified body
no longer bound
by physical limitations
time, space, walls

an imperfect body
bearing wounds
marked by love
hands, feet, side

wounds,
a remembrance of
the price of love
and cruel world realities

but wounds also
a spring of love
grace instilling hope
pain will not dissuade God's love

wounds empowering a fragile doubting faith

Spend some time reflecting on the truth that Jesus' glorified body still bears the wounds of the crucifixion. How do the visible wounds help Thomas? What does this tell us about God's ability to use our wounds? How might your own wounds be possible portals of love, empathy and compassion?

JESUS' WOUNDS AND OURS

(JOHN 20:24-29)

Jesus' wounds remain—
a needed message for Thomas
and of great significance for us.

God's love shining through
the wounds of Jesus
vibrant crimson, even beautiful.

A vivid reminder that
all wounds this side of heaven
are not fully healed.

That our wounds too
can be a conduit of hope
nurturing another's faith.

For our remaining wounds speak louder
than any well-intended wishes
or perfunctory prayers.

When touched or scarred by pain,
we bring our anger, doubts, fears,
to God with unedited honesty,

eventually finding a level of comfort,
even a tentative hope
from God who is with us in our pain.

God's love shining through our wounds,
offers an essential message of faith
to a doubting, broken world.

What are your struggles in being cared for? Is it difficult to be vulnerable, to allow yourself to feel the fullness of pain and hurt? How have you received God's comfort when wounded by life's circumstances? What did you learn about the character of God during those times? Ask God to help you be a gracious, loving, safe presence to others struggling through difficult times.

Do You Love Me?

(John 21:15-19)

The risen Jesus appears to the
sword-swinging, thrice-denying Peter,
a needed yet uncomfortable encounter.

Jesus seeks not an apology,
not correct doctrinal ascent,
not even extraordinary faith.

Jesus plunges into the heart of the matter,
with a thrice-repeated question
cutting Peter to the quick,
splaying his heart.

Three times a single question is posed
each iteration of the question
slicing deeper and deeper
with the skill of an accomplished surgeon.

Do you love me more than these?
Do you love me?
Do you love me?
Three questions recalling
three previous denials.

Peter, bewildered and spent,
"You know all things, Lord
you know I love you"—
only now Peter knows it too!

The demon exorcized, Peter reconciled,
Jesus extends the familiar invitation,
"Follow me."

Three times Peter denied Jesus, and three times Jesus asked the same question. How do you think Peter felt about this conversation? Is there anything right now that you and Jesus need to talk through? What in your life competes with your love for Jesus? How is the Lord Jesus inviting you to partner with God, cooperate with what God is doing even with your shortcomings?

PAST/PRESENT FAITH

(JOHN 14:12, 16:7)

Once again, the rules apply:
one loaf = one loaf
one fish = one fish.
Jesus dead, risen, gone.

Faith looking backwards
for inspiration, solace—
belief fixed to past events.

Testimonies to what was—
water to wine, blind gained sight,
lame danced, prisoners freed,
storms calmed, thousands fed.

The flowing river of following Jesus
now a stagnant pond, past stories
told again and again, vibrant faith
now faded like an old photo—

until the tongues of fire,
the coming of the Spirit, the
promised One now arrived,

faith made alive; fresh and flowing,
God within, the wind blowing—
new wine, new wineskins,

new stories, new exploits, new life,
a present faith and future hope,
Jesus fleshed out, real-time encounters—
"greater things you shall do."

At times we look to our distant past to recall something Jesus did in our lives. Take some time now to think through what God has been doing in you and through you recently. How do you currently see God at work? Ask God to make you more aware in order to be a better partner with God.

LET JESUS GO

How drawn I am to Jesus—
My friend, brother, shepherd,
who tires, hungers, sleeps,
is tempted, suffers, weeps.

But that Jesus is no more.
Transformed through suffering,
death, resurrection—
seated at the right hand,
glorified, exalted, almighty,
the Christ, powerful, mystery,
Alpha and Omega.

Described poetically by John,
though indescribable God/man,
knowing human experience,
temptation, suffering, pain.
God with us, within us, praying for us,
His prayers informed by living among us.

Jesus the Christ—God with us,
King of Kings, Lord of Lords,
Alive, the Living One.
Letting go of the God-man,
we open to the mystery
of new life found,
new life hidden in Christ.

How do you feel about the person of Jesus before His resurrection? What feelings arise as you change your focus to the risen, glorified Christ figuratively described in Revelation 1:12-18? How is each manifestation of Jesus a gift? How might both be helpful in bringing you comfort, fostering trust in difficult times? What might Jesus' prayers be for you today as Jesus walks with you and lives within you?

DEATH TO LIFE

(LUKE 9:23-24)

Cross-carrying
self-denying
no looking back
seeking first God's Kingdom
not-my-will-but-God's-will-be-done life

not an end in itself but
nurturing a new beginning—
denial, suffering, death
ushering in resurrection.

Bringing New life
    Eternal
        Full
            Fruit-bearing
              Familial
                Joy-laced
                  Love-saturated
                    Grace-guzzling
                      Forgiveness-flowing life

free from self—
to love, to serve,
to live, to be
seeking God's kingdom,
God's-will-be-done-
on-earth-
as-it-is-in-heaven life.

Denial of self and the resurrection life are not in opposition to one another, but form and inform one another. What are the possible dangers of over-emphasizing one aspect to the exclusion of the other? Which aspect of the Christian life—denial or fullness of life—is your primary focus? Why? How are you currently experiencing the resurrection life?

MAKING A MASTERPIECE

(EPHESIANS 2:10)

The Artist hovers
above the empty canvas,
love pulsating,
increasing in intensity.

Unable to be contained,
love erupts
in creative energy.
The canvas void no more.

The Sculptor molds and shapes
the final pieces,
fashioned from the earth—
male and female.

The Poet breathes life
into this masterpiece,
this uncanny expression of
Artist, Sculptor and Poet.

You are this canvas, this sculpture, this poem—
an outpouring of love's creative activity,
containing and embodying the Divine,
fueled and sustained by love.

Embrace the wonder of who you are, the masterpiece of the Triune God. How is God inviting you to be more comfortable with yourself as a divinely created masterpiece? Choose one of these designations (canvas, sculpture, poem) to carry with you today, reminding yourself from time to time of your identity—the wonder of who you are.

Stop, Look and Listen

Having reached the end of this section, take some time to go back and review your journal using one or more of the prompts below. You may want to do this over a few days.

Word/Phrase

Write the words/phrases/questions that stood out to you in the previous reflections, thoughts that drew you in or caused resistance, affected you positively or negatively, moved you in some way. Try using different colored pens to represent different emotions. Pay attention to and make note of your feelings, listening for the invitations or challenges from God.

Exploring Themes

Attempt to discover what message(s) God has for you. What might God be inviting or challenging you to embrace, live into? If a particular theme surfaces, consider the nature of it. Is it more of an invitation (something you long for and welcome) or a challenge (something to overcome)?

What do you notice about Jesus through these poems and questions? Does anything surprise you? How might your feelings toward or your experience of Jesus be shifting, expanding, deepening?

Writing Poetry

Now that your journey through this book has come to an end, take some time to write a poem that expresses a major theme(s) from each of the three sections. Choose a familiar gospel passage you enjoy and rewrite it as a free verse poem.

You can do this. You don't need to complete it today—take your time and have some fun. Leave it for a while and come back to it another day. Take poetic license with the story and the verse; freely create, as God, the creator and loving parent, delights in your efforts.

APPENDIX: POEMS FOR HOLY WEEK

The following poems are compiled to provide a source of meditation for each day of Holy Week, beginning with Palm Sunday.

Index of Select Themes

Identity

Judging

Loving Others

Seeing Eyes/Hearing Ears

Seeing Jesus with New Eyes

Silence and Solitude

Suffering

Treasure

Scripture Index

Acknowledgments

Once again, I was able to assemble the same team (plus one) that I worked with on my last two books. Three trusted and highly prized, hugely creative, and exceptionally capable individuals whom I have learned to trust and depend on over the last three years. I am privileged and honored by their willingness to continue this journey of writing with me. Especially this time around, as the style of writing was quite different. Their agreement to partner with me freed me to create and write, knowing they would help form and shape what I had written into something readable and helpful.

First off, I would like to thank Gail Steel. Gail is a trusted friend and is invaluable. This time around she stepped up in a big way: encouraging, challenging, rewriting and declaring in no uncertain terms her perspective on a number of poems—the ones she liked and those she did not like. She pushed back and boldly proclaimed her thoughts with honesty and frankness, working hard to make this offering something we all could be proud of. If you happen to come across something a tad bit uncouth, do not blame her (I had final say); instead take solace in the fact that it could have been much worse without her dogged efforts! Once again, Gail's presence was/is a gift from God to me. She went above and beyond what I had dared to hope for, smoothing out some rough edges and de-cheesing some of those cheesy passages I so love to write.

Secondly, I want to thank Jessica Snell, my trusted editor. I was unsure that she would take on this project because it is poetic in nature and thus the punctuation is not very straightforward (and Jessica loves her some punctuation!). But thankfully she took on the project and did a wonderful job of bringing punctuational consistency to a number of the poems, asking some good questions, and taking this to the next level. She is a wonderful gift and the first person I mention when I hear someone needs an editor. I know whatever I give her will be returned in much better shape and I so appreciate her attention to detail. She is a fantastic editor.

This brings me the final member of the trio: Christine Smith, an accomplished artist who continues to say yes when I ask her to design a cover for me. If you saw the covers of the first two books she did for me—*Discernment, God's Will & Living Jesus* and *Journey with Grief*—you know the spectacular work she does. You can't judge a book by its cover, but striking covers can help entice people to explore the inside of a book and her covers do just that.

Finally, this year I invited one more person to join me on this project and that was Melissa Romero (aka Misty). One day Misty made an extraordinary declaration in my presence regarding her ability to ask good questions. A statement I did not doubt. So I asked her to present suggested questions for each of the 117 poems, which she agreed to do and she somehow managed to get them done within my timeframe while also managing a household, a husband, three kids, and traveling back east for an extended time. Her work was extremely helpful and I hope this experience may prime the pump for her own writing project in the not-too-distant future.

As you can see, this book you hold in your hands would not exist in its present form without the dedicated and inspired efforts of four marvelous people. Once again, I can attest to the faithfulness of God, who provides what one needs to accomplish that which God invites one to put one's hand to.

Thank you, Gail, Jessica, Christine and Misty.

OTHER BOOKS BY LARRY WARNER

Journey with Jesus: Discovering the Spiritual Exercises of Saint Ignatius (Downers Grove: InterVarsity Press, 2010).

Discernment, God's Will & Living Jesus: Christian Discernment as a Way of Life (Oceanside: barefooted publishing, 2016).

Journey with Grief: Navigating the First Year (Oceanside: barefooted publishing, 2018).

Made in the USA
Columbia, SC
19 November 2019